IMAGES
of America

JEWISH
LOS ANGELES

IMAGES
of America

JEWISH
LOS ANGELES

Jonathan L. Friedmann

ARCADIA
PUBLISHING

Published by Arcadia Publishing
Charleston, South Carolina

Printed in the United States of America

Library of Congress Control Number: 2020932391

For all general information, please contact Arcadia Publishing:
Telephone 843-853-2070
Fax 843-853-0044
E-mail sales@arcadiapublishing.com
For customer service and orders:
Toll-Free 1-888-313-2665

Visit us on the Internet at www.arcadiapublishing.com

CONTENTS

ACKNOWLEDGMENTS

The Western States Jewish History Association began as an offshoot of the Southern California Jewish Historical Society, a local branch of the American Jewish Historical Society. In 1968, Dr. Norton Stern (1920–1992), the association's founder, established the journal *Western States Jewish Historical Quarterly*, which later became *Western States Jewish History*. For over 50 years, the association and journal have collected materials and disseminated research pertaining to the experiences of Jews in the Western United States. Dr. Stern was joined by his longtime collaborator, Rabbi William M. Kramer (1920–2004), who maintained the archives and published the journal after Stern's death in 1992. This book is indebted to their extensive collection of photographs, advertisements, newspaper articles, government records, family histories, political membership lists, receipts, letters, diaries, interviews, posters, business cards, and more. David W. Epstein (publisher and managing editor) and Gladys Sturman (publisher and editor-in-chief) took over the journal and archives in 1998. After their retirement in late 2018, David asked me to succeed him as president of the Western States Jewish History Association, editor of *Western States Jewish History*, and director of the Jewish Museum of the American West (established in 2013), an online museum of more than 600 exhibits. I am grateful to David for giving me this opportunity and to John F. Guest, who joined me as the association's vice president.

Thank you to Erin L. Vosgien, acquisitions editor at Arcadia Publishing, and to Caroline Anderson, title manager at Arcadia, for guiding this book through the stages of production. I am most thankful for my wife, Elvia, who makes everything I do possible.

All images reproduced in this book are from the Western States Jewish History Association Archives.

INTRODUCTION

When California entered the Union in 1850, the census listed just eight Jews living in Los Angeles. By 1855, the fledgling city had a Hebrew Benevolent Society and a Jewish cemetery. Congregation B'nai B'rith (now Wilshire Boulevard Temple), the city's first Jewish congregation, was formed in 1862. Meanwhile, Jewish merchants, bankers, and business owners helped found the chamber of commerce, Masonic order, library association, Odd Fellows order, Turnverein (German American athletics club), and other Jewish and nonsectarian organizations. Jewish property owners developed vast areas of Los Angeles and beyond into neighborhoods and cities we know today. By 1897, the city's Jewish population was large enough to support its own newspaper, *B'nai B'rith Messenger*.

The 20th century witnessed rapid growth in the city and its Jewish community. Numerous synagogues and community centers emerged in the sprawling landscape, serving Jewish residents of various rites, denominations, and cultural backgrounds. When *B'nai B'rith Messenger* began publishing in January 1897, the population of Los Angeles was around 100,000, and Jews numbered under 3,000. By the time it ceased publication in 1995, the city had increased to over 3,000,000, with Jews exceeding 500,000. Today, Los Angeles has the fourth largest Jewish population in the world, after Tel Aviv, New York City, and Jerusalem.

The Jewish history of Los Angeles exemplifies the experience of Jews in the American West. Unlike those who stayed in Europe or on the East Coast, Western Jews were inclined to start anew rather than repeat patterns of the past. Geographically distant from traditional spheres of influence, Los Angeles Jews were not beholden to established norms or expectations. Rabbi Leonard Beerman, who arrived in Los Angeles in the 1950s, spoke for many who came before and after him: "This was a place not known for following everybody else. A place where somebody like me could come along, stir things up, and not get kicked out."

Western Jews in the early years tended to be less religious, or at least less meticulous about adhering to ancient folkways. Los Angeles was without a kosher market or formal congregation until 1862. Most Jewish residents only attended services during the High Holidays (Rosh Hashanah and Yom Kippur), and a benevolent society was formed almost two decades before the city's first synagogue building was erected.

Antisemitism was rare in the Western states during the 19th and early 20th centuries. As newcomers to a dusty outpost that was home to a multiethnic mixture of other newcomers, Mexicans, and Native Americans, Jews largely evaded prejudices that followed them elsewhere. Los Angeles Jews were elected to public office at nearly every level, despite forming an insignificant part of the electorate, and filled the ranks of civic groups, private clubs, and elite circles. This atmosphere of tolerance was undermined in later decades, as bigotry and xenophobia accompanied the Immigration Act of 1924, the Great Depression, the rise of Nazism, increased migration from the Midwest and Northeast, and the Red Scare following World War II. Nevertheless, Los Angeles Jewry as a whole remained upwardly mobile, owing to the city's rapid industrialization, access to public higher education, the growth of Hollywood, and New Deal initiatives.

Jewish life in the American West was also decentralized. By the 1870s, eighty-four percent of Western Jews lived in California, mostly due to the Gold Rush. However, Jews were not concentrated in a single spot. They settled in more cities, towns, and neighborhoods in California than anywhere else in the Union. The unstructured environment gave them almost instant certification as Americans and afforded them opportunities to develop their lives and livelihoods in an open land of seemingly endless opportunities.

Civic commitment was another hallmark of Los Angeles's pioneer Jewish community. Jews were often the first to create communal organizations and helped found charities, hospitals, libraries, and fraternal lodges. The Hebrew Benevolent Society (established in 1854) was the city's first chartered charitable organization, and the Ladies' Hebrew Benevolent Society (established in 1870) was its first women's charity. Other important Jewish institutions included Kaspare Cohn Hospital (today's Cedars-Sinai Medical Center, established in 1902), the Jewish Orphans Home of Southern California (today's Vista Del Mar Child and Family Services, established in 1908), and the Jewish Consumptive Relief Association (today's City of Hope National Medical Center, established in 1913).

Los Angeles Jews also engaged in interreligious cooperation earlier than Jews in other parts of the country. These included mutual efforts in education, social welfare, commerce, and progressive reform. For example, prominent Jews helped raise funds for the city's first institute of higher learning, St. Vincent's College (established in 1865), which gradually evolved into the Jesuit Loyola Marymount University.

The images in this book depict Jewish life in Los Angeles from its beginnings in the 1840s to its expansion in the 1950s. Because of the long timeframe and the large population involved, this photographic history is, by necessity, representative rather than comprehensive. Numerous individuals, institutions, and organizations have been left out, either to make room for others or, more often, because photographs were not available in our archives. This is most obvious in the book's inclusion of Jews in the film, music, and television industries. These subjects are only lightly touched upon and deserve a volume of their own.

The stories contained in the captions are likewise only glimpses. For over 50 years, the Los Angeles area has been a central focus of the Western States Jewish History Association, its journal *Western States Jewish History*, and its online Jewish Museum of the American West. Readers are encouraged to explore these resources to learn more about the industrious and enterprising Jews who helped shape Los Angeles into the metropolis it is today.

One

1840s–1850s

When the first Jewish settler arrived in the Pueblo de Los Ángeles in 1841, the town had little more than 1,000 residents. The US victory in the Mexican-American War, the California Gold Rush of 1849, and the granting of California statehood in 1850 brought an influx of pioneers to the state, most of whom settled in the northern regions. By 1860, an estimated 10,000 Jews had reached California from the East Coast and Europe, about half of whom settled in San Francisco. Many others set up shops and businesses in boomtowns throughout the Gold Country. Only a handful found their way to Los Angeles. The 1850 census recorded just eight recognizably Jewish names among the 1,610 inhabitants counted in Los Angeles. All eight were unmarried men, seven were merchants, one was a tailor, six were from Germany, one was from Poland, and one came from Portland, Oregon. As Gold Rush prosperity trickled southwards, Jewish merchants began arriving in Los Angeles from San Francisco, the Eastern United States, and directly from Central and Western Europe. The city's first lay rabbi arrived in 1854, and the Los Angeles Hebrew Benevolent Society was formed later that year. A Jewish cemetery was consecrated in 1855 at Chavez Ravine, near the current site of Dodger Stadium. Meanwhile, Jewish pioneers became active in local politics, fraternal lodges, charities, commerce, and real estate.

1	2	3	4	5	6	
		Bernada	25	f	I	
		Jacob Frankford	40	m	I[1]	Tailor
92	92	Morris Michael	19	m		Merch
		A Jacoba	25	m		Do
93	93	Augustin Wasserman	24	m		Do
		Felix Pachman	28	m		Do
94	94	Timothy Foster	41	m		Do
		John F Simmons	30	m		Farme
		David Douglass	30	m		Trade
		Julia	45	f	B	
95	95	Phillip Sichel	28	m		Merch
		Joseph Plumer	24	m		Do
		Goodman	24	m		Do
96	96	Maria Guadaloupe Urea	66	f		
		Maria Moreno	47	f		
		Bautisto	29	m		
97	97	Pedro Seis	29	m		Restau
		José Utimio Maguanes	25	m		Cook
		Francisco Lamas	40	m		Do

The first known Jewish settler in the Mexican Pueblo de Los Ángeles was Jacob Frankfort, a German-born tailor who arrived in 1841 as part of the Rowland-Workman exploratory party traveling west from Santa Fe, New Mexico. Jacob was among eight Jewish men recorded in Los Angeles in the 1850 census, taken shortly after California was admitted to the Union. Jacob, whose last name was misprinted as "Frankford," later made his home in San Francisco.

Jacob Frankfort opened a tailor business and men's clothing store in a corner shop in Bell's Row, a two-story adobe building at the southeast corner of Aliso and Los Angeles Streets. Built in 1845 by Capt. Alexander Bell, the building was later sold to Henry Mellus and renamed Mellus Row. Each of the eight Jewish Angelinos listed in the 1850 census worked and lived in Bell's Row.

Bavarian-born Morris L. Goodman became a US citizen in Cincinnati in 1843. After a short stint in New York, Morris arrived in Los Angeles in 1849 and worked as a dry goods merchant in Bell's Row. In 1850, Morris served on the inaugural Common Council of Los Angeles. He later partnered in the property investment firm of Rimpau, Fritze & Company and formed the general merchandise firm of Goodman & Rimpau. In 1872, Morris led a group of German immigrants to settle in the Southern California city of Anaheim, seen in this 1880s photograph.

Jacob Elias arrived in Los Angeles with his two brothers, Raphael and Israel, in 1851 or 1852. They opened Elias Bros. dry goods in the Temple Block, pictured here, which is the current site of Los Angeles City Hall. Jacob acquired 35 plots in today's Hollywood, and in 1860, he purchased Rancho San Rafael, now the city of Glendale. He was the founding secretary and treasurer of the Los Angeles Hebrew Benevolent Society, and in 1854, he wrote the petition for Jewish cemetery land at Chavez Ravine.

11

Born Louis Galefsky in the Polish province of Posen, Louis Phillips became a naturalized citizen in Los Angeles in 1851 (formalized in 1852), making him among the first Jews to become US citizens in California. A successful rancher, Louis purchased a 2,400-acre portion of the San Antonio Ranch, along the San Gabriel River, which now comprises the cities of Huntington Park, Lynwood, Vernon, Maywood, Bell, South Gate, and Montebello. He acquired more land as the years went on. In 1864, Louis purchased 12,000 acres of the old Rancho San Jose land grant in northeastern Los Angeles County. The Phillips Mansion, now operated by the Historical Society of Pomona Valley, was built on the site in 1875. Louis sold most of the surrounding acreage for subdivision into the Pomona Tract, thus beginning the city of Pomona.

In addition to ranch land, Louis Phillips owned Los Angeles properties and built a number of downtown buildings, including Phillips Block No. 1 in the heart of the business district. The building, considered Los Angeles's first skyscraper, would house the original Hamburger's Department Store, known as the People's Store. Other Phillips Blocks had hotels, restaurants, and assorted businesses.

Joseph P. Newmark left Prussia for New York City in 1848. He traveled to Kentucky and back to New York before arriving in Los Angeles around 1852. After opening a clothing store with Jacob Rich, Joseph invited his younger brother, Harris Newmark, to leave Prussia and join the business. The Newmark brothers partnered with Maurice Kremer and their uncle, Joseph Newmark, to form Newmark, Kremer & Company, a wholesale-retail dry goods store.

Tiring of the dry goods business, Joseph P. Newmark soon left Newmark, Kremer & Company for San Francisco, where he worked as a commission broker of merchandise. Joseph married Augusta Leseritz in Posen in 1855 and brought her back to San Francisco. They had seven children, including Leo, pictured here, who became a leading medical doctor.

A native of Loebau, Prussia, Harris Newmark traveled Europe with his father, Philip Newmark, selling printer's ink. Harris arrived in Los Angeles in 1853 and briefly clerked at his brother Joseph P. Newmark's wholesale clothing store. Harris continued in the clothing business until 1861, when his interests turned to hides and wool.

When Harris Newmark's uncle, Joseph Newmark, arrived in Los Angeles in 1854, young Harris moved in with him. Harris learned English from his aunt, Rosa Newmark. On March 16, 1858, Harris married his cousin, Sarah Newmark, the daughter of Joseph and Rosa. The bride's father performed the ceremony.

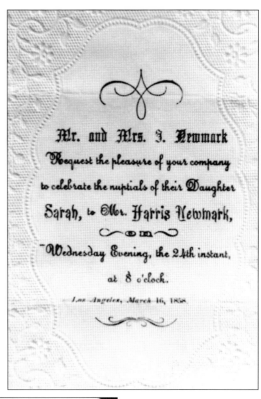

Mr. and Mrs. J. Newmark
Request the pleasure of your company
to celebrate the nuptials of their Daughter
Sarah, to Mr. Harris Newmark,
on
Wednesday Evening, the 24th instant,
at 8 o'clock.

Los Angeles, March 16, 1858.

In 1877, Harris Newmark purchased the Temple Block, a three-story building at Temple and Main Streets. Harris Newmark's building stood between two larger buildings. Daniel Desmond's store, which later expanded into Desmond's department stores, was to the left of Newmark's building. Jacoby Bros., another major retailer, occupied the larger building on the right.

Harris Newmark was one of three advisors of the Ladies' Hebrew Benevolent Society. Through the years, he served as president of Congregation B'nai B'rith; helped found the Los Angeles Public Library, Los Angeles Board of Trade, and Southwest Museum (now part of the Autry Museum of the American West); was a charter member of the Los Angeles Chamber of Commerce; and supported the Jewish Orphans Home of Southern California (now Vista del Mar Child and Family Services). Harris had the honor of digging the first shovel of dirt at the ground-breaking of the Jewish Orphans Home.

Marco (left) and Maurice Newmark (right), sons of Harris Newmark, coedited their father's landmark memoir, *Sixty Years in Southern California, 1853–1913* (1919). The book is among the most valuable firsthand accounts of 19th-century Southern California. The brothers re-edited the book for its second edition in 1926, and Marco edited the final edition in 1930 (Maurice died in 1929).

In the early 1850s, German native Ernestine Greenbaum became the first Jewish women to settle in Los Angeles. By the early 1870s, she was operating a boardinghouse and had a reputation as "a motherly friend to many a young and homeless Jewish boy seeking his fortune in the West" (Max Vorspan and Lloyd P. Gartner, *History of the Jewish of Los Angeles*, page 35).

Ephraim Greenbaum and his wife, Ernestine, opened the White House Hotel in 1875. They were soon joined by a Mrs. Goldstein, who previously operated a boardinghouse and a fruit, candy, and cigar stand. Ephraim and Ernestine also may have been the parents of the first Anglo child born in Los Angeles.

Solomon Lazard left Alsace, France, for New York in 1844. He worked for his cousins' business, Lazard Frères, then a leading import-export house and today a French banking giant. In 1851, after working at Lazard Frères stores in Northern California, Solomon purchased a stock of goods, intending to open his own business in San Diego. He instead settled in Los Angeles, where he had a shop in Bell's Row. Following a brief partnership with another cousin, Maurice Kremer, Solomon set off on his own as S. Lazard & Company, eventually building a brick store on Main Street—one of the city's first fireproof buildings.

In 1869, Solomon Lazard, John S. Griffen, and Prudence Beaudry took over Los Angeles's failing water company, receiving a 30-year lease from the city. With Solomon as president, the Los Angeles Water Company established a major water supply system using iron pipes. When the lease expired, the city bought back the water company and developed it into the Los Angeles Department of Water and Power. This undershot waterwheel, built in 1861, lifted water into an elevated flume and delivered it to a reservoir north of the old Catholic cemetery.

Following his arrival in America, Maurice Kremer, a native of Alsace, France, found his way to Memphis, Tennessee. In 1852, he journeyed to Los Angeles, where he partnered with his cousin, Solomon Lazard, to form the dry goods firm of Lazard & Kremer Company. In 1856, Maurice joined with his father-in-law Joseph Newmark, Joseph P. Newmark, and Harris Newmark in Newmark, Kremer & Company, a wholesale-retail dry goods company. Maurice later opened M. Kremer & Company, a fruit shipping company for farmers. In 1889, he entered the insurance business, and he sold fire insurance until his death in 1907. Maurice was married to Matilda Newmark, a daughter of Joseph Newmark. They had 12 children, but only six survived infancy.

Maurice Kremer distinguished himself as a civic and Jewish leader in Los Angeles. He served as city treasurer, school board member, tax collector, and trustee of the Hebrew Benevolent Society, and he helped found the French Benevolent Society, Turnverein (German American athletics club), Home of Peace Cemetery, and Temple Union Sewing Circle, which made clothes for the poor and needy. Maurice's wife, Matilda, was a charter vice president of the Ladies' Hebrew Benevolent Society of Los Angeles.

John Jones was born to Polish parents in Poland or London in the early 1800s. Around the age of 38, he was sentenced at the Old Bailey in London to life in prison for stealing a breast pin. He was sent to a penal colony in Australia and received his certificate of freedom seven years later. News of the California Gold Rush brought him to San Francisco in 1850. A few years later, he was operating a wholesale business in Los Angeles.

John Jones returned to San Francisco in the mid-1850s and served as vice president of Congregation Shearith Israel. By 1863, he was again in Los Angeles. He partnered in a wholesale food company with Bernard Cohn that dissolved in 1871 when Cohn joined with Hellman, Hass & Company. That same year, John became the first Jew to serve as president of the Los Angeles City Council (then known as the common council).

In the late 1850s, John Jones married Doria Deighton, a Scottish-born Christian, in San Francisco. When the Ladies' Hebrew Benevolent Society of Los Angeles was formed in 1870 as the city's first women's charity, Doria was elected treasurer. During the 1870s, John and Doria became land owners and developers. Doria continued the venture after John's death in 1876 and was instrumental in developing Los Angeles's inner city.

German-born Samuel Prager arrived in Los Angeles with his brother Charles in 1854. The brothers were active in Los Angeles Masonic Lodge No. 42, which attracted a number of influential Jewish pioneers, including Rabbi Abraham Wolf Edelman, Isaias W. Hellman, and Harris Newmark. Samuel, pictured here, operated a dry goods and furniture store and was one of the original oil salesmen in Los Angeles. In the days before automobiles, oil was used for covering dirt streets and lubricating machinery and was refined for lamp oil.

Samuel Prager married Rosalie Loewenstein of San Diego. The couple had eight children—five boys and three girls. George M. Cohan, the popular composer of "Yankee Doodle Dandy" and over 300 other songs, was a friend of Rosalie's nephew Mannie Loewenstein. Cohan frequently dined at the Prager home.

Solomon Nunes Carvalho, an artist and photographer of Spanish-Portuguese Jewish descent, was born in Charleston, South Carolina, in 1815. By 1853, Solomon had photography and painting galleries in Baltimore, Philadelphia, and New York City. In the winter of 1853–1854, he was hired as a photographer for John Charles Frémont's Fifth Expedition, which journeyed through Kansas, Colorado, and Utah in search of a railroad route to the Pacific Ocean. Solomon arrived in Los Angeles in 1854, taking up residence and establishing his studio on the second floor of La Tienda de China, a fancy dry goods store on Main Street operated by two Sephardic brothers, Samuel K. and Joseph I. Labatt. The brothers joined Solomon in forming the Hebrew Benevolent Society (established in 1854, now Jewish Family Service), the city's first chartered nonprofit charitable organization.

Abraham Lincoln and Diogenes, from around 1865, is Solomon Nunes Carvalho's best-known work. The 44-by-34-inch oil painting depicts the Greek Cynic philosopher Diogenes dropping his lantern upon encountering Lincoln, surprised that he had at last found an honest man—the subject of his legendary quest. Lincoln, seated beneath a neoclassical statue of George Washington, holds a copy of his second inaugural address open to the words "malice toward none, with charity for all."

Samuel K. Labatt, a Sephardic Jew from North Carolina, had been active in the New Orleans Hebrew Benevolent Society before heading west for Los Angeles with his brother Joseph. The brothers' successful Main Street store, La Tienda de China, soon moved to a larger brick building, also on Main Street, where it specialized in "Fancy Dry Goods, Gent's Furnishings, $20,000 Worth of Jewelry, Gold Watches, and Accordions." Samuel and Joseph left Los Angeles for San Francisco in 1855, and Samuel later relocated to Texas.

Joseph Newmark, a Prussian-born *schochet* (ritual slaughterer), arrived in New York City in 1824; he helped found that city's first Ashkenazi congregation, B'nai Jeshurun, in 1825. Joseph and his wife, Rosa, arrived in San Francisco in 1852, and two years later, they moved south to Los Angeles. Joseph entered the wholesale-retail dry goods business of Newmark, Kremer & Company and was a founder of the Hebrew Benevolent Society. He acted as the lay rabbi of Los Angeles until 1862, when he invited Rabbi Abraham Wolf Edelman to lead the newly formed Congregation B'nai B'rith (today's Wilshire Boulevard Temple).

London-born Rosa Levy married Joseph Newmark in New York in 1835. Rosa was the driving force behind the Ladies' Hebrew Benevolent Society in Los Angeles, founded in 1870, although she never accepted a position in the society. The society "alleviated distress, nursing the sick back to health, burying the dead with all the sacred ceremonies and comforting the afflicted ones with their sympathy" (Norton B. Stern, *The Jews of Los Angeles*, page 102).

Joseph and Rosa Newmark had six children, five of whom are pictured here: Edward, Sarah, Caroline, Harriet, and Matilda. The other son, Meyer J. Newmark, was elected Los Angeles city attorney in 1862 and was the first Jew to hold that office. The Newmark family was related to the core of Los Angeles's early Jewish pioneers: Sarah married her cousin Harris Newmark, Harriet married Eugene Meyer, and Caroline married Solomon Lazard.

The Hebrew Benevolent Society of Los Angeles established a Jewish cemetery in 1855 at Lilac Terrace and Lookout Drive in Chavez Ravine. The cemetery fulfilled the society's goal of "procuring a piece of ground suitable for the purpose of a burying ground for the deceased of their own faith, and also to appropriate a portion of their time and means to the holy cause of benevolence" (Constitution and By-Laws of the Hebrew Benevolent Society of Los Angeles, 1855).

This photograph was taken at the Jewish cemetery at Chavez Ravine around 1900. The man in the center is likely Rabbi Abraham Wolf Edelman, the city's first official rabbi.

On Saturdays, the children of the cemetery's non-Jewish superintendent, Oscar Willenberg, had the chore of sweeping and tidying the site. The property was sold on October 27, 1902, and between 1902 and 1910, the interred were moved to Home of Peace Cemetery in East Los Angeles, run by Congregation B'nai B'rith. Chavez Ravine became the site of Dodger Stadium in 1959.

Bert

Dick

S.-W. Corner 9ᵗʰ and Main St.

"Marsh-Strong Building"
(Now stands on this Corner.)

B. W. Trowbridge
—driver—

Wm. E. Stoermer
—engineer—

Jim Richards
—driver—

Jim Simmer
—foreman—

In 1852, sixteen-year-old Bernard Cohn left Prussian-occupied Poland for New York City. He arrived in Los Angeles three years later and clerked in the store of Isaac Schlesinger, located in Bell's Row. Within two years, Bernard had his own dry goods store and, when that proved unsuccessful, a brokerage business. Gold discoveries in the Arizona Territory in 1862 prompted Bernard to set up a general merchandise business there, partnering with Joseph and Michael Goldwater (Michael was the grandfather of politician Barry Goldwater). After the Goldwaters bought out Bernard's share in the company, he returned to Los Angeles and entered the food business with John Jones. Among his involvements in Los Angeles, Bernard was elected to the city council, serving as chairman and mayor pro tempore after the mayor's untimely death, and was a member of the Confidence Engine Company No. 2 volunteer fire department, pictured here. (Bernard Cohn is not shown in this photograph).

Born in Russian-occupied Poland, Wolf Kalisher received his US citizenship papers in Los Angeles in 1855. He had a store at Bell's Row and in the 1860s purchased a quarter section of Rancho Santa Gertrude, comprising 800 acres and an adobe house. Today, that area includes the cities of Downey and Santa Fe Springs in southeast Los Angeles County. As a merchant, Kalisher was noted for hiring local Indians as workers and household help and for assisting Indians with their disputes. In September 1874, H.C. Hubbard, a landowner in the San Fernando Valley, requested that a street in Granada Hills be named for Kalisher. In 1995, the San Fernando City Council proposed changing the street's name to honor labor leader Cesar Chavez. The proposal was abandoned after residents argued that Kalisher had done for Indians what Chavez had done for Hispanic laborers.

Henry Wartenberg, a Prussian-born Jewish and civic leader, came to Los Angeles in 1857. He partnered with Wolf Kalisher in a general merchandise store in Bell's Row, and together they formed Los Angeles Pioneer Tannery, the city's first leather tanning factory. During the 1860s, Henry served on the County Grand Jury and Los Angeles City Council and founded the local Democratic Club. He was also the founding president of the city's first volunteer fire department and Gan Eden Lodge No. 8 of Kesher Shel Barzel (Band of Iron), a national Jewish fraternity, among other civic and communal roles. He is interred at the Home of Peace Cemetery.

Leaving his native Germany to avoid the draft, Herman W. Hellman settled in Los Angeles in 1859. He drove a mail stage before clerking for his uncle Samuel Hellman in his stationery, book, dry goods, and cigar store. Shortly after becoming a partner in that business, Herman left to establish Hellman, Haas & Company, which by the 1880s was recognized as the largest wholesale grocer in the Southwest.

In 1890, Herman W. Hellman's older brother, Isaias W. Hellman, took over California's largest bank, the Nevada-California Bank, which necessitated his move from Los Angeles to San Francisco. Isaias recruited Herman as vice president and general manager of the Los Angeles Farmers & Merchants Bank. Herman purchased this stately home on South Hill Street.

Herman W. Hellman was heavily invested in real estate in the Los Angeles area. In addition to his mansion on South Hill Street, he owned 20 acres in Alhambra, and in 1903, he built an eight-story office building on Fourth and Spring Streets that still stands today.

At the invitation of his cousin Harris Newmark, Kaspare Cohn immigrated to America from Prussia and arrived in Los Angeles in 1859. Kaspare worked at Harris's store and slept on the premises before opening his own crockery business in the Northern California town of Red Bluff. He returned to Los Angeles in 1866, establishing a grocery and dry goods wholesale-retail business, H. Newmark & Company, with his brother Samuel Cohn and Harris Newmark. He later partnered in another firm with Harris and Morris A. Newmark. Kaspare also formed K. Cohn & Company, specializing in the collection and shipping of hides and wool, and in 1896, he helped create the Pacific Wool Company, which processed wool in "the most modern of ways." Kaspare was involved in real estate, banking, and utilities ventures and was instrumental in shaping what would become the Home of Peace Cemetery, Vista Del Mar Child and Family Services, City of Hope National Medical Center, Cedars-Sinai Medical Center, and other institutions. In 1914, he founded the Kaspare Cohn Commercial & Savings Bank, which developed into Union Bank.

Isaias W. Hellman arrived in Los Angeles with his younger brother Herman in 1859. Isaias opened a dry goods store in 1865. His honest reputation led some customers to leave their excess gold and silver with him for safekeeping. He converted part of his store into an unofficial bank, complete with printed deposit slips. In 1868, Isaias was part of Los Angeles's first official bank, Hellman, Temple & Company, and in 1871 he founded the Farmers & Merchants Bank.

Isaias W. Hellman married Esther Newgass of New York in 1870. Esther's sister, Babette, was married to Mayer Lehman, one of the founders of Lehman Brothers, thus bringing Isaias into the family of New York bankers. Isaias and Esther had three children: Isaias William Hellman Jr., Clara, and Florence.

This 1880s lithograph shows the Isaias W. Hellman residence on Main and Fourth Streets. Isaias was a major landowner in Southern California, with holdings comprising numerous city lots and swaths of former rancho land. Isaias and a syndicate purchased Rancho Cucamonga in 1871 and, later, Rancho Los Alamitos, both in their entirety. Along with William Workman, he owned much of the Boyle Heights neighborhood, and with Harris Newmark, he owned part of Repetto Ranch (today's Montebello). Isaias was influential in bringing the Southern Pacific Railroad to Los Angeles in 1876, and in 1879, he contributed land for the founding of the University of Southern California. Isaias left Los Angeles in 1890 for San Francisco, where he served as president of the Nevada Bank and nationalized the bank as Nevada National Bank of San Francisco. In 1905, he bought the banking division of Wells Fargo and merged it with the Nevada National Bank, creating Wells Fargo Nevada National Bank of San Francisco, which later became Wells Fargo Bank.

Two

1860s–1870s

Between 1860 and 1870, the population of Los Angeles grew from 4,385 to 5,728 residents, among them 330 Jews. Although the total number was small, the proportion of Jews compared to the general population, 5.76 percent, exceeded that of New York City at the time. By 1876, the Jewish population of Los Angeles increased to about 600. This period of growth brought important institutional developments. The city's first kosher meat market was opened in 1862. That same year, the mostly German Congregation B'nai B'rith was formed, replacing the short-lived Polish Jewish congregation, Beth El, which started in 1861. B'nai B'rith constructed the city's first synagogue building in 1873. The Ladies' Hebrew Benevolent Society was founded in 1870, and the Los Angeles chapter of the Independent Order of B'nai B'rith began in 1874. Jews held elected office, started banking operations, and expanded their business ventures. An 1873 editorial in the local *Daily News* summed up the Jews' welcome contributions to the city: "We commend them for their commercial integrity and their studied isolation from prevalent vices of gambling and inebriation. We commend them for their general business and personal probity. . . . They are among our best citizens and the city suffers nothing in their hands."

A native of Alsace, France, Eugene Meyer came to Los Angeles in 1861 and worked in a dry goods store owned by his cousin Solomon Lazard. Eugene eventually bought the store with his brother, Constant Meyer, and enlarged it into City of Paris (Ville de Paris). The store carried sporting goods, housewares, shoes, toiletries, cameras, luggage, umbrellas, and clothing. Eugene Meyer also served as French consul in Los Angeles and was a founding member of the Los Angeles Board of Trade (today's chamber of commerce).

City of Paris, the leading dry goods store in Los Angeles, moved into an impressive building that was constructed in 1880 on South Broadway. Proprietor Eugene Meyer relocated to San Francisco in 1883 to become the West Coast manager of Lazard Frères, which supplied thousands of miners in the Gold Country. Ten years later, he moved to New York City to head the company.

In 1867, Eugene Meyer married Harriet Newmark, the daughter of Joseph Newmark. They had eight children. Their son Eugene Meyer Jr. worked for Lazard Frères and later cofounded Allied Chemical & Dye, served as chairman of the Federal Reserve (1930–1933), and owned the *Washington Post* (1933–1946). His sister Katharine Meyer Graham ran the *Washington Post* for years.

In 1872, the City of Los Angeles approved Eugene Meyer's request for a section of the City Cemetery to be allocated for members of the French Benevolent Society, which he served as president: "Your petitioners, the officers and members of the French Benevolent Society, respectfully petition your honorable body, for a plot of ground in the city cemetery, in which to bury their members, similar to the plots given or sold to the Masons and Odd Fellows. We hope that your honorable body will consider our petition favorably."

Leopold Harris left Prussia for America in 1852, settling briefly in Louisville, Kentucky, where his brother resided. He then headed to California, engaging in business ventures in San Francisco, San Gabriel, and San Bernardino before arriving in Los Angeles in the early 1860s. In 1870, Leopold took over a Main Street stationery store formerly operated by Herman W. Hellman, and by the 1880s, he owned Quincy Hall Clothing Company. Leopold also operated the wholesale menswear firm of L. Harris & Company.

L. Harris & Company became Harris & Frank when Herman W. Frank, a highly trusted manager within Leopold Harris's business, married Harris's daughter. By 1903, the business was being run by Herman W. Frank, Harris's son Harry, and another son-in-law, M.C. Adler.

Congregation B'nai B'rith, today's Wilshire Boulevard Temple, received its charter from the State of California in 1862, making it the city's third religious congregation. Before that time, Jewish services were held in various locations and were often conducted by Joseph Newmark, a successful businessman and lay rabbi. The originally Orthodox congregation rented locations until 1873, when it occupied its own Gothic structure at the corner of Temple Street and Broadway.

Rabbi Abraham Wolf Edelman was born in Poland in 1832 and immigrated to America in 1851 with his wife, Hannah Pessah Cohn. Eight years later, they were living in San Francisco, where Abraham studied, taught Hebrew, and sold dry goods. Joseph Newmark, an organizer and lay rabbi of Los Angeles's Jewish community, persuaded Rabbi Edelman to come to Los Angeles and serve as its first fulltime Jewish spiritual leader. Edelman served Congregation B'nai B'rith from its inception in 1862 to 1885.

Abraham and Hannah Pessah Edelman had six children: Rachel, Matilda, Benjamin, Abraham M., Henry W., and David W. After Abraham left Congregation B'nai B'rith, the family lived off of his real estate holdings, including property at the corner of Sixth and Main Streets, where he erected a multistory building.

The bar mitzvah of David W. Edelman, son of Abraham and Hannah, was commemorated at Congregation B'nai B'rith on February 11, 1882. David would go on to study medicine at Columbia University and become the first Los Angeles–born Jewish doctor. In 1929, when Congregation B'nai B'rith became known as Wilshire Boulevard Temple, David served as its president. In later years, he was chief of staff at Cedars of Lebanon Hospital (now Cedars-Sinai Medical Center).

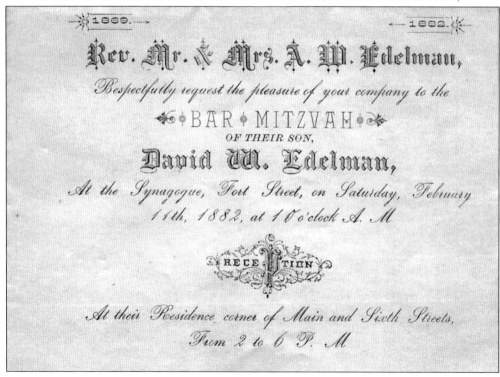

Esther Hellman, the wife of banker Isaias W. Helman, donated a curtain for the ark holding the Torah scrolls at Congregation B'nai B'rith. The Los Angeles *Daily Evening Republican* reported on April 14, 1876, "The conclusion of the Feast of Passover will be the next Sunday. Rev. Mr. [Abraham W.] Edelman will preach at 10 o'clock, his theme being 'The Perpetual Light.' During the services a curtain for the Holy Ark, presented by Mrs. Isaias W. Hellman, will be consecrated. This is described as one of the most magnificent pieces of church ornamentation in California and is a credit to the liberality of Mrs. Hellman." The *chuppah* (marriage canopy) in front of the ark was made for the first double wedding at the synagogue in December 1885. The couples were Ella Newmark and Carl Seligman and Jeannette Lazard and Louis Lewin. The brides were first cousins.

Abraham Haas, a native of Bavaria, arrived in Los Angeles in 1864 at the age of 17. In 1867, he entered into a wholesale-retail grocery store with his brother Jacob Haas, Herman W. Hellman, and Bernard Cohn. Hellman, Hass & Company was located on Los Angeles Street, across from H. Newmark & Company. The store sold everything from medicine to explosives.

Hellman, Haas & Company was one of seven names in the first Los Angeles phone directory. From his share in the company, Abraham Haas launched one of the first flour milling and cold storage businesses in Los Angeles, along with several electricity and gas companies—forerunners of current Southern California power companies.

In the 1880s, Herman W. Hellman left Hellman, Haas & Company to take over management of Farmers & Merchants Bank. The firm changed to Haas, Baruch & Company and grew into the city's preeminent wholesale grocer. Haas, Baruch & Company eventually morphed into the Smart & Final grocery chain.

In 1862, H.M. Cohn, a sheep grazer, partnered with Leopold Harris in the first kosher butcher shop in Los Angeles. The scarcity of kosher meat was a problem for observant Jews throughout the American West. This photograph shows Temple Street around 1865.

Jewish pioneers supported a variety of Roman Catholic charitable projects in early Los Angeles, including the city's first orphanage, improvements to the Catholic cemetery, renovations of the first church, and construction of the cathedral. Prominent Angelinos met in May 1865 to plan St. Vincent's College, the first institute of higher learning in Southern California, which occupied a block bounded by Broadway, Sixth Street, Hill Street, and Seventh Street. Today, the site is known as St. Vincent Court, in the heart of the jewelry district. Rosa Newmark, wife of Joseph Newmark, spearheaded efforts to raise funds for the planned college. Led by Vincentians since its founding, the college changed hands to the Jesuits in 1911. St. Vincent's gradually grew into Loyola Marymount University, located in the Westchester neighborhood of Los Angeles.

Isaac Lankershim, a native of Bavaria, arrived in America as a teenager in 1836. He first settled in St. Louis, Missouri, where he learned the grain and livestock shipping trades. He applied those trades in various regions of California before coming to Los Angeles in the late 1860s. Despite being baptized in St. Louis prior to marrying English-born Annis Lydia Moore, Isaac retained close business and social ties to Harris Newmark and other Los Angeles Jewish businessmen. In 1869, Isaac joined investors from San Francisco in purchasing 60,000 acres in the San Fernando Valley and forming the San Fernando Valley Farm Homestead Association. The expansive ranch, which was first used to raise sheep and was later converted into wheat fields, comprised today's Woodland Hills, Tarzana, Encino, Sherman Oaks, Van Nuys, and North Hollywood.

Prussian-born Louis Lewin arrived in Los Angeles with his brother-in-law A. David Hirshfield in 1868. Louis opened a stationery and office supply store, with Pincus Lazarus as a limited partner, and in 1876 published *Centennial History of Los Angeles* (by Jonathan T. Warner, Benjamin Hayes, and Joseph Widney), the first history of the county.

Simon Nordlinger was born in Alsace, near the Swiss border, and apprenticed as a Swiss watchmaker before making his way to Los Angeles in 1869. Simon acquired a watchmaking business at 3 Commercial Street, between Main and Los Angeles Streets. He began with a small stock of watches, some inexpensive jewelry displayed in a window, and a large wooden watch hung outside as a sign. He lived in the rear of his store.

In the early 1870s, Simon Nordlinger's watch and jewelry store moved around the corner to Main Street. By 1886, Simon was occupying a larger store at 130 Main Street, where he added jewelry manufacturing and gold- and silversmithing. The business remained in the family until 1923.

German Jews in America joined with other German immigrants in forming turnvereins, local chapters of an international cultural and athletic fraternal organization. The Los Angeles turnverein began taking shape around 1870 and helped German Jews attain far greater equality with other Germans than was possible in their homeland.

Prussian-born Emil Harris settled in Los Angeles in 1869. He soon became a gymnastics instructor and rifle team member at the turnverein and was recognized as a champion marksman of Southern California. In 1870, Harris became one of just six Los Angeles policemen. He conversed with Jewish merchants in Yiddish and kept watch over their stores. During the Chinese Massacre riots of 1871, Emil did his best to protect the Chinese from the anti-Chinese mob. In 1874, he led the posse that captured robber-murderer Tiburcio Vásquez, who was threatening Los Angeles. Emil was appointed chief of police in 1878 and later started his own private detective agency, becoming one of city's first private eyes. Emil and his younger brother, Max Harris, were instrumental in founding the Young Men's Hebrew Association of Los Angeles in 1887.

Leopold Harris and Charles Jacoby were Prussian-born proprietors of Harris & Jacoby, a general merchandise store at 63 Main Street, pictured here in 1871. In December 1873, the store advertised its "Christmas and New Year Novelties," noting that "Santa Claus will hold sway during the season and goods will be offered at excessively low rates!"

Los Angeles, 1865.
Bella Union Hotel

Rabbi Hyam Zvee Sneersohn, a Russian-born resident of Jerusalem, arrived in America in 1869 for an 18-month lecture tour, during which he was introduced to Pres. Ulysses S. Grant. Rabbi Sneersohn arrived in Los Angeles in late July 1870 and stayed at the Bella Union Hotel on North Main Street, the former site of the last capitol building of Mexican California. Rabbi Sneersohn remained in Los Angeles long enough to be counted in the 1870 census.

A native of Moudon, Switzerland, Eugene Germain arrived in New York City in 1868 and soon after headed west. He operated supply stores along the Southern Pacific Railroad in Texas, New Mexico, and Arizona before opening a restaurant in Los Angeles in 1870. Eugene next entered the poultry business, eventually developing Germain Fruit Company, specializing in seed and nursery stock.

In 1889, Eugene Germain renamed his business Germain Seed & Plant Company. Eugene was a two-term president of the Los Angeles Board of Trade and the first vice president of the reactivated Los Angeles Chamber of Commerce, and he served for four years as US consul to Zurich, Switzerland, under Pres. Grover Cleveland.

German-born Pincus Lazarus settled in New York City and Tucson, Arizona, before arriving in 1874 in Los Angeles, where he entered the stationery business with Louis Lewin. In 1882, Pincus married Rachel Kremer, the daughter of Maurice Kremer. He later established his own firm, Lazarus Stationery Company.

Founded in New York in 1843, the Independent Order of B'nai B'rith came to Los Angeles in 1874. Isidor N. Choynski, a well-known San Francisco newspaper writer and book dealer, visited Los Angeles to help form Orange Lodge No. 224 of the Jewish fraternal organization. The lodge's first two presidents were Samuel Prager and Rabbi Abraham Wolf Edelman.

In 1871, brothers Joseph, David, and Lazard Coblentz left the Lorraine region of France, on the German border, to avoid being drafted into the Prussian army. By 1874, David and Joseph Coblentz had settled in Los Angeles, where they entered the wholesale liquor business. Joseph partnered with his wife's uncle, Michel Levy, to form the Levy & Coblentz liquor firm.

During the 1870s and 1880s, Levy & Coblentz occupied a prime location in the Downey Block at the corner of Spring and Temple Streets, in the heart of the city's business district. Levy & Coblentz is seen at the far left of this 1875 photograph.

פ נ

חלבון בן ר׳ שמואל
על אלה אני בוכיה
עיני עיני ירדו מים
אל האיש הישר ישינ
בק הי
לכל הן בים קטו אייר
ש תרלה ל ג נ צ ב ה

In memory of
GEORGE KALLMAN
a native of Prussia
Died May 20, 1875.
Aged 39 years.

In the early morning of May 20, 1875, Simon Goldsmith prepared to ride horseback to Los Angeles from Rincon, near the Los Angeles County line, for the purpose of attending his brother's wedding. Simon's business partner, George Kallman, arose to see him off. Just before departing, Simon took a large sum of the firm's money, evidently to pay bills in Los Angeles. George protested, perhaps fearing the common occurrence of robberies along the route, which took several hours to travel. According to an account in the *Los Angeles Express*, "a violent dispute ensued, which ended in Kallman striking Goldsmith with a bridle. Goldsmith instantly drew his pistol and fired, three shots, some say, killing Kallman." George Kallman was buried at the Jewish cemetery at Chavez Ravine later that day.

Max Meyberg left Germany for America, settling briefly in New York City and San Francisco before coming to Los Angeles in 1875. Max and his brother, Moritz, operated the Crystal Palace, a successful crockery and giftware store.

The Crystal Palace store on Main Street opened in 1887. The *Los Angeles Herald* described the opening as "an event which will long be remembered by those who attended, attracted thither by the brilliant lights, the excellent music and the beautiful new wares which were displayed in tasteful array upon the shelves. The firm of Meyberg Bros. is well and favorably known to all residents of Los Angeles and throughout the East, and is composed of Mr. Max Meyberg and Mr. Moritz Meyberg."

Max Meyberg was married to Emma Hellman, a daughter of Isaiah M. Hellman of the Los Angeles banking family. The interior of their home is pictured here. Max is best remembered for creating La Fiesta de Los Angeles, a parade and street festival in downtown Los Angeles, in April 1894. The festival began as a way to attract tourists during a time of business recession and to rival the Tournament of Roses Parade in Pasadena, which debuted four years earlier. The festival was held annually until 1916.

The Jacoby family of Loebau, Prussia, arrived in America at different times during the 1870s. Five brothers settled in Los Angeles: Isaac, pictured here, Nathan, Charles, Abraham, and Lessor. Another brother, Herman, also came to California but settled in Wilmington, in the Los Angeles Harbor region, where he became postmaster.

In 1878, the five Jacoby brothers established a business in the Temple Block, selling a full line of clothing, furnishing goods, boots, shoes, hats, and more. Jacoby Bros. operated at both wholesale and retail levels, with 30 salesmen in the store and three traveling salesmen.

Jacoby Bros. soon expanded to larger and larger locations, becoming one of the leading firms in Los Angeles. In the early 1930s, the company was sold to David May of the May Company of St. Louis, Missouri.

Three

1880s–1890s

Between 1880 and 1890, the population of Los Angeles rose sharply from 11,183 to 50,395. This fivefold increase was aided by the arrival of transcontinental rail service (Southern Pacific Railroad in 1881 and Santa Fe Railroad in 1885) and aggressive promotions from the chamber of commerce, the *Los Angeles Times*, the Los Angeles Merchants Association, citrus growers, and other industries. The Los Angeles Telephone Company began offering service in 1881. In 1882, the California Electric Light Company (later Los Angeles Electric Company) began providing electricity for the city's new streetlights. Within a year, Los Angeles became the first US city to completely abandon gas lamps for electric street lighting. Attracted by these modern marvels and promotional campaigns, the new residents, largely from the Midwest, changed social patterns in the Jewish community. Whereas earlier decades were characterized by integration and close collaborations between Jews and non-Jews, imported prejudices caused many Jews to turn inward and form separate social groups, such as the Concordia Club (established in 1891). The Jewish community was also served by its own newspaper, *B'nai B'rith Messenger*, beginning in 1897.

Asher Hamburger, a native of Bavaria, arrived in New York City in 1839. He worked in a tassel factory before starting a small general store in Pennsylvania. He next relocated with two brothers to Alabama, where they opened stores along the Tombigbee River. In 1850, the California Gold Rush drew them west to Sacramento, where Asher stayed after his brothers left for San Francisco. Despite fires and floods, Asher kept the Sacramento store going with his sons, David and Moses, who finally convinced their father to move to Los Angeles in 1881.

The Hamburger family called their first establishment the People's Store, a 20-by-75-foot room on Main Street near Requena Street that catered to working-class customers. One year later, the store moved to Temple and Spring Streets, in the Bumiller Block. Later it moved into the newly built Phillips Block, pictured here.

The Hamburger Building, constructed in 1908 at 801 South Broadway, housed Hamburger's Department Store. The structure was designed by Alfred F. Rosenheim, a leading early-20th-century Los Angeles architect whose other major projects included the Hellman Building, the Second Church of Christ Scientist, and the Eugene W. Britt House. The Beaux Arts–style Hamburger Building was the city's largest modern steel-frame building, with 1.1 million square feet spanning over 10 floors, and was the largest department store west of Chicago. The south end of the building featured Hamburger's Majestic Theatre, built for full stage shows and opera. In 1924, Hamburger's was sold in to David May of the May Company of St. Louis, Missouri. Now known as the Broadway Trade Center, the underutilized building is being developed into a mixed-use complex that will include offices, a hotel, retail space, restaurants, and a food hall.

TROY SHIRT FACTORY,

Adolph Seligman, Prop'r.

Shirts and Underwear

MADE TO ORDER IN ANY STYLE.

Room 24, Schumacher Block, Opp. Post-Office,

LOS ANGELES, CAL.

P. O. BOX 106. (OVER)

Adolph Seligman's Troy Shirt Factory was located in the Schumacher factory on North Spring Street. The back of this early 1880s advertisement card lists an assortment of made-to-order shirts, including white, colored, spotted, striped, linen, cotton, flannel, cassimere, open-front, open-back, with and without cuffs, with and without collars, "any kind of shirt," and "any other kind of shirt."

Rose Loeb Levi, the Los Angeles–born daughter of Leon Loeb and Estelle Newmark Loeb, was educated at Marlborough School, a college preparatory school, and graduated from the Girls Collegiate School. At age 18, Rose married 31-year-old German native Herman Levi. Rose was an expert on Shakespeare and the Bible and often had philosophical discussions with Rabbi Edgar F. Magnin of Congregation B'nai B'rith. She is pictured here in her engagement dress, which she wore at a reception for Pres. William McKinley in 1901.

John Newmark Levi Sr., the son of Rose and Herman Levi, was an executive at Capitol Milling Company, a flour milling business in downtown Los Angeles. Established in 1883, the company was owned and operated by the Levi and Loew families. An advertisement from 1905 boasted, "Every run of Capitol Flour is tested every day for its strength and nutritive value. Every user of Capitol Flour will find that in cases of indigestion, cases of diabetes, [and] cases of failing strength great benefit will be derived from Capitol Flour. It has the nutriment to build and nourish, to supply bone, muscle, blood and brain. Every sack guaranteed." Capitol Milling was the city's oldest family-owned business when it was sold 1999. Its five-building complex at 1231 North Spring Street includes some of the oldest extant buildings in Los Angeles.

Herman W. Frank arrived in Los Angeles from Walla Walla, Washington, in 1887, and began working for Leopold Harris in his clothing retail business. When Herman became a partner in the company the following year, the name was changed from London Clothing Company to Harris & Frank. The first Harris & Frank store was at the southwest corner of Spring and Temple Streets. It was among the first Los Angeles stores to feature a "Christmas effect," with holiday decorations and window displays to lure in customers. In addition to being business partners, Herman became Leopold's son-in-law when he married his daughter Sarah Harris. Herman continued to run the business following Leopold's death in 1910 and retired in 1927. He returned to Harris & Frank in 1934 to help the business through the Great Depression.

Herman W. Frank married Sarah Harris, Leopold's daughter, in 1888. Soon after, Leopold made his new son-in-law general manager of their business. Herman and Sarah had two sons, one of whom, Lawrence, helped found the Jewish Big Brothers Association of Los Angeles in 1916. Community service ran in the family. Herman Frank was treasurer of Congregation B'nai B'rith, president of the Los Angeles Board of Education, and president of United Charities, the forerunner of the United Fund.

In 1886, Londoner Al Levy partnered in two ill-fated San Francisco restaurants before settling in Los Angeles, a city with few quality eateries. He operated an oyster bar pushcart, selling the popular delicacies to patrons of the Grand Opera House and other theaters. The oysters were imported from San Francisco, which required re-icing four times on the trip by train.

Al Levy's pushcart evolved into the Oyster House on Fifth and Spring Streets, later the site of the Alexandria Hotel. His second and larger restaurant, located at Third and Main Streets, became a center of fashionable night life in the early 1900s. A third site on Spring Street, between Seventh and Eighth Streets, was complete with large banquet rooms, such as the one pictured here. This was followed by Al Levy's Tavern on North Vine Street.

Herman Silver left Prussian Saxony for North America in 1848. He spent several years in Montreal, New York, Illinois, and Colorado before coming to Los Angeles in 1887 at the urging of his doctor, who was concerned about Herman's "congestion of the lungs." At the time, Herman was the secretary and treasurer of the Atchison, Topeka & Santa Fe Railroad. He was granted a franchise for a cable railroad in Los Angeles and was appointed receiver of the Los Angeles & Pacific Railway.

In 1896, Herman Silver was elected to the Los Angeles City Council and was voted in as president, sometimes acting as the mayor pro tem. When the Lazard, Beaudry, and Griffith lease on the Los Angeles Water Company ended in 1899, the city council created a water commission and made Herman its chairman. He initiated a reservoir project northeast of downtown that combined stored water with a development of homes and parks. The area became known as Silver Lake in his honor.

Mannie (Emanuel) Loewenstein (left) is pictured with his friend George M. Cohan, the acclaimed composer, playwright, and entertainer. Mannie's father, Hilliard, arrived in Los Angeles from Loebau, Prussia, in 1852, and was a partner in Samuel Meyer's dry goods business. Hilliard saw a photograph of Samuel's sister, Rosa Meyer, and in 1856 traveled to Strassburg, Prussia, to marry her. They remained in Europe for two years, where Mannie was born in 1857.

German-born Herman H. Goldschmidt came to Los Angeles in 1888 to avoid being drafted into military service. Herman developed a liquor business with his brother, Max Goldschmidt, who had arrived in Los Angeles in 1886. Herman also purchased real estate throughout Southern California, including acreage in Simi Valley, two ranches in Riverside County, beach land in Huntington Beach, vineyards in Cucamonga, and land that is today San Clemente.

The third rabbi of Congregation B'nai B'rith was Rabbi Abraham Blum, a native of Alsace, France. Rabbi Blum was trained at the rabbinical school in Niederbronn in northeastern France, graduating at the age of 17. After immigrating to America in 1866, he served synagogues in Ohio and Galveston, Texas, where he also received a medical degree from a local college. Rabbi Blum arrived in Los Angeles in 1889 and served B'nai B'rith until 1895.

On May 25, 1889, Annie Cohn, the daughter of Los Angeles pawnbroker Leopold B. Cohn, married non-Jew Edward W. Kinney, the driver for Fire Engine Company No. 4. After the civil ceremony, Edward visited Annie's father Leopold B. Cohn. Leopold was heartbroken over the escapade, and a stormy scene ensued. Peace was restored when, eight days later, Edward became the first person to convert to Judaism in Los Angeles. Rabbi Abraham Blum of Congregation B'nai B'rith oversaw the process, which included a crash course in Judaism and a ritual circumcision. Immediately after the conversion, the couple was again married, this time in a Jewish ceremony conducted by Rabbi Abraham Blum. Local newspaper headings the next morning read, "Ed Kinney Accepts the Faith of His Charming Bride"; "Joins the Jewish Church"; and "A Newly Wedded Man Embraces the Jewish Faith."

In May 1891, the Concordia Club of Los Angeles was incorporated for the "social and mental culture" of its Jewish membership. The club quickly attracted 100 members drawn from the city's most prosperous Jewish families. Meetings were held at the former Elks Club until 1894, when the club secured rented quarters at the luxurious Burbank Theater Building on Main Street. This photograph shows club members performing Sydney Rosenfeld's one-act comedic play *Off the Stage* in 1894.

During the 1890s, school teaching was one of the few careers considered suitable for daughters of pioneer Jewish families. A handful elected to attend state teacher training institutions, called normal schools, including Jeannette Lazard (pictured here), Emma Fleishman, Bertha Marx, and sisters Mina and Esther Norton.

Jeannette Lazard was a daughter of Solomon Lazard, one of the early Jewish settlers in Los Angeles. Jeanette taught at Laurel Canyon School and was married to Louis Lewin, who operated a stationery store. Their one daughter, Rosa Leontine Lewin, died just two days shy of her first birthday.

Sisters Mina and Esther Norton graduated from the California State Normal School in Los Angeles in 1894, which later became the University of California, Los Angeles (established in 1919). Mina, shown here, taught for a year at the newly opened Santa Monica Canyon School and then taught at the Ann Street School. According to family lore, one of Mina's students was Leo Carrillo, the celebrated actor and conservationist for whom Leo Carrillo State Park in Malibu is named.

Presented

To

By

19

Alfred Arndt, a Russian-born Jewish religious functionary, settled in Toledo, Ohio, before moving to Los Angeles in 1895. He floated from position to position, including brief stints as rabbi of Kahal Israel, a small Orthodox synagogue, principal of the Hebrew Free School, and High Holiday rabbi for Congregation Beth Israel (a merger of Kahal Israel and Beth El). Alfred also tried to make it as an author, self-publishing *The Secrets of Happiness and Longevity; or, How to be Happy and Live Longer* (1903), a compendium of essays and quotations from noted authorities. From 1904 to 1907, Alfred was again involved at Beth Israel, this time as cantor and teacher at the synagogue's *cheder* (elementary school), and occasionally as "reverend." He proposed the establishment of a Hebrew university in Los Angeles in 1907, which went nowhere. In 1915, Alfred became the first rabbi of Mosaic Law Congregation in Sacramento, California.

In 1893, Prussian-born rabbi Moses G. Solomon graduated from both the University of Cincinnati and Hebrew Union College in Cincinnati. Two years later, he was hired as the fourth rabbi of Congregation B'nai B'rith in Los Angeles. Under Rabbi Solomon, the congregation adopted the Reform movement's *Union Prayer Book*.

Congregation B'nai B'rith built its second synagogue in 1895 at Ninth and Hope Streets. The building was designed by Abraham M. Edelman, the son of the congregation's first rabbi, Abraham Wolf Edelman, and featured the largest chandelier in the city. The new building was dedicated in front of a capacity crowd of Jews and Christians.

Isaac O. Levy, the youngest son of liquor salesman Michel Levy, was one of a group of teenagers involved in the Young Men's Hebrew Association under the auspices of Rabbi Moses G. Solomon. In 1896, the group consisted of 14 boys in their late teens, 12 of whom are pictured here. From left to right are (first row) Henry M. Newmark, Isaac O. Levy, George N. Black, Albert M. Norton, Edgard Baruch, Robert Newmark, and Samuel T. Norton; (second row) Abraham Kremer, Samuel Behrendt, Marco H. Hellman, Leo W. Barnett, and Isaiah M. Norton. Most of these boys remained active in the city's Jewish community as adults. Isaac O. Levy later partnered with Samuel Behrendt in the Behrendt-Levy Insurance Agency.

Lionel L. Edwards, a 24-year-old native of San Francisco, founded Los Angeles's first Jewish newspaper in 1897. Originally called the *Emanu-El*, copying its name from the San Francisco paper founded by Rabbi Jacob Voorsanger of Congregation Emanu-El, the masthead was changed to *B'nai B'rith Messenger* on April 15, 1898, linking it with Los Angeles's leading synagogue, Congregation B'nai B'rith. Initially a bimonthly publication, *B'nai B'rith Messenger* chronicled the growth of the city and its Jewish population, including reports on local meetings, lectures, visits from national and international figures, the hiring and firing of rabbis and community leaders, and the development of Jewish institutions. The paper supported Zionism and the settling of Eastern European Jews in Mexico rather than in California. Before 1917, the paper urged American neutrality in World War I, arguing that European countries on both sides of the war espoused antisemitism. *B'nai B'rith Messenger* became a weekly in the 1920s.

B'nai B'rith Messenger continued publishing in various forms for nearly a century. Leonard Leader, a reporter and sometime editor of the newspaper, described the *Messenger's* significance: "There is no better and consistent record of the origins, growth, and development of the second largest Jewish community in the United States." Lionel Edwards's office is shown here in 1901.

Editor Victor Harris was the guiding force behind *B'nai B'rith Messenger* from 1897 to 1929. The newspaper became an essential resource for the city's Jews and Jewish institutions. In 1898, the *Messenger's* directory included Congregation B'nai B'rith, Kahal Israel, the Hebrew Benevolent Society, the Concordia Club, and the Independent Order of B'nai B'rith Orange Lodge and Semi-Tropic Lodge. The list grew significantly as the decades went on.

In 1898, Chicago-born conductor and bandleader Abraham Frankum Frankenstein became the first permanent theater orchestra director in Los Angeles, taking the helm at the Orpheum Theatre on South Main Street. He remained at the theater for over 30 years. Abraham cowrote California's state song, "I Love You, California" (1913), with lyricist S.B. Silverwood of Silverwood's men's clothing store in downtown Los Angeles. Abraham also organized bands for the Los Angeles Fire and Police Departments.

Daniel J. Brownstein and his eventual business partner, Henry W.D. Louis, worked for Jacoby Bros. men's clothing store in Los Angeles in the early 1890s. By 1898, the two men joined with Philip Newmark in Brownstein, Newmark & Louis, manufacturing work clothes and specializing in overalls. The company was the first in Los Angeles with a unionized garment shop. In 1910, Philip Newmark left Brownstein, Newmark & Louis to start his own firm. Brownstein-Louis Company was incorporated later that year.

Hungarian-born Rabbi Sigmund Hecht served congregations in Alabama and Wisconsin before assuming the rabbinic post at Congregation B'nai B'rith (1899–1919). As the congregation's fifth rabbi, he helped expand programming for women and young people and oversaw the creation of Home of Peace Cemetery in East Los Angeles. Rabbi Hecht also authored *Post-Biblical History: A Compendium of Jewish History from the Close of the Biblical Records to the Present Day* (1896).

Bavarian-born Abraham Mooser joined the Confederate army in 1861, while living in Mississippi, and was wounded four times at the Battle of Shiloh. In the late 1880s, Abraham and his growing family arrived in Los Angeles, where he started a grocery business. By the early 1890s, Abraham had a general merchandise store in Santa Monica on Third and Utah Streets (now Broadway). This 1899 photograph commemorates the 25th wedding anniversary of Abraham and Henrietta Mooser (left), joined by their six children and five grandchildren.

Four

1900s–1920s

During the early decades of the 20th century, Los Angeles achieved its status as the "southern metropolis." In 1900, the population was 102,479—double what it had been just 10 years earlier. By 1920, the city had exploded to 576,673. The Jewish population outpaced the larger trend, growing from approximately 2,500 in 1900 to about 40,000 in 1920. Numerous factors contributed to the city's rapid growth, including the San Francisco earthquake of 1906, which sent migrants southwards, the emergence of the Hollywood film industry, and emigration from Europe following World War I. The Industrial Removal Office in New York brought some 2,000 Eastern European Jews to Los Angeles. Some Jews became pioneers of the nascent movie business. Others started businesses to accommodate the city's growing customer base. The multi-ethnic Boyle Heights neighborhood attracted many Jewish residents. The Temple Street and Central Avenue districts also became Jewish neighborhoods. The list of Jewish institutions grew to include Kaspare Cohn Hospital (today's Cedars-Sinai Medical Center), Jewish Consumptive Relief Association (today's City of Hope National Medical Center), Hebrew Sheltering Home for the Aged (today's Jewish Home), Jewish Orphans Home of Southern California (today's Vista Del Mar Child and Family Services), National Council of Jewish Women, Young Zionist Association, and several others. The Federation of Jewish Charities was formed in 1912 to unite fundraising efforts of the various organizations.

By the turn of the 20th century, the Jewish cemetery at Chavez Ravine was no longer able to serve the city's growing Jewish population. Between 1902 and 1910, the interred were transferred to Home of Peace, a new cemetery on Stephenson Avenue (now Whittier Boulevard) in East Los Angeles established by Congregation B'nai B'rith. A house was built on the grounds of the cemetery for the superintendent and his family.

A low spot at the Home of Peace Cemetery was developed into a small pond that collected excess water from the watered lawns. Although the grounds were maintained by Congregation B'nai B'rith, a report from 1902 stipulated that "plots will be sold to other Jewish societies, and provision has been made for the proper burial of indigent Jews."

The Orthodox Congregation Beth Israel dedicated its synagogue on Olive Street in 1902. Also known as the Olive Street Shul, the building housed the Beth Israel Hebrew School (Talmud Torah), organized by the ladies' auxiliary. In 1906, the congregation purchased cemetery land on Downey Road.

The wedding of H. Lew Zuckerman and Sadie Belle Goldberg took place at the Olive Street Shul on February 28, 1909. Rabbi Isidore Myers of Sinai Temple officiated, with assistance from M.A. Alter and Alfred Arndt. This is the only known interior view of the Olive Street Shul. The *Los Angeles Times* noted that the photograph was "the first known to be taken of an Orthodox Jewish ceremony in a synagogue."

In 1902, Kaspare Cohn donated a two-story Victorian home at 1441 Carroll Avenue to the Hebrew Benevolent Society. The home served as a free hospital for Jewish patients with tuberculosis. In 1910, a second Kaspare Cohn Hospital was built on Stephenson Avenue (now Whittier Boulevard), near Boyle Heights, for general care. A third hospital was built in 1930 on Fountain Avenue in the Hollywood area and was known as Cedars of Lebanon. In 1961, the hospital merged with Mount Sinai Hospital to became Cedars-Sinai Medical Center, which opened its current building in 1976.

In 1905, Dr. Sarah Vasen was hired as the superintendent and resident physician of the Kaspare Cohn Hospital on Carroll Avenue. A native of Quincy, Illinois, Sarah was the first Jewish woman to practice medicine in Los Angeles.

Solomon Kinderman and Rose Rosenbloom were married in San Bernardino, California, in 1902. The couple relocated to Los Angeles and opened a wholesale clothing and secondhand store. Tragically, Solomon, pictured on the left with his brother-in-law Henry Rosenbloom, was shot and killed in the store. A "spectacular gun battle" ensued, as reported in the *Los Angeles Herald* on May 27, 1918: "The gun battle occurred when Ventura Rodriguez, 26, a Mexican laborer, shot and killed Solomon Kinderman, a North Main Street pawnbroker. Rodriguez exchanged shots with Patrolmen Teddy McAuliffe, F. Condaffer, J.E. Davis and P.H. Button. Patrolmen McAuliffe was shot in the left foot. Patrolman Condaffer was shot in the left arm. The bullet fractured a bone. Margarito Soto, a bystander, was shot in the right leg."

Breslau-born Julius R. Black was brought to Los Angeles in 1875, where he was educated in public schools. Julius worked in Mexico City from 1896 to 1902, at which time he returned to Los Angeles to engage in a real estate and investment firm with his brother George. Julius was active in B'nai B'rith Lodge No. 487.

Polish-born Simon F. Norton settled in Los Angeles in 1878 and formed a downtown dry goods business with his cousins. About a decade later, Henry Klein, a native of Trebišov in eastern Slovakia (then part of Hungary), opened the Star Clothing Company at the corner of First and Main Streets, giving Simon some serious competition. In August 1896, Henry Klein married Simon's daughter, Mamie. The two families established a joint business, Klein-Norton Company, in 1903.

The Klein-Norton Company wholesale store on South Los Angeles Street is seen here in 1918. The company specialized in shirts, hosiery, underwear, union suits, and overalls, and advertised as a seller of "Mens' and Ladies' Furnishing Goods and Notions."

Chicago native Louis M. Cole spent several years in California's San Joaquin Valley before moving south to Los Angeles in 1903, where he engaged in insurance, real estate, and warehousing. When the cornerstone of the Shrine Auditorium (pictured here) was laid in 1915, Louis was president of the Al Malaikah Shriners. He also served as president of the B'nai B'rith Lodge in 1919.

Dr. Sanford Zuckermon,

SURGEON CHIROPODIST

·ọ· ·ọ̈· ·ọ·

All Ailments of the Feet successfully treated without pain.

WITH
IMPERIAL HAIR BAZAAR
AT HAMMAM BATHS ────────

OFFICE HOURS:
9 A. M. to 12 M.
1 P. M. to 5 P. M.

TELEPHONE Black 691.

210 S. BROADWAY,   LOS ANGELES, CAL.

During the late 19th and early 20th centuries, a substantial number of chiropodists (now better known as podiatrists) were women. Dr. Zuckermon is listed as "Miss Sanford Zuckermon" in the Los Angeles city directory. Her practice was situated in the Imperial Hair Bazaar, operated by Frank Neubauer.

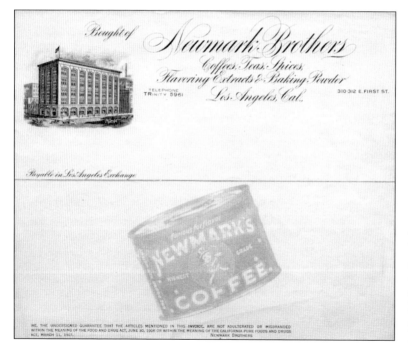

Samuel M. Newmark, the son of Joseph P. Newmark, ran a thriving coffee business during the early part of the 20th century. Newmark Bros. occupied a five-story brick building at the corner of First and San Pedro Streets designed by Alfred F. Rosenheim, one of the city's leading architects.

Born near Coburg, Germany, Jacob Stern spent time in New York City and Cleveland, Ohio, before joining his cousin Joseph Goodman in 1889 in a Fullerton, California, merchandise business. Stern & Goodman Mercantile grew into five Southern California stores and was one of the state's first chain stores. In 1904, Jacob moved his family to Hollywood and entered the real estate business. His office was located in downtown Los Angeles in the Pacific Electric Building on Main Street.

Jacob Stern married Sarah Levanthal in 1891. Sarah's father, Elias Levanthal, was among the founding members of the Hebrew Benevolent Society of Los Angeles (established in 1854). Prior to marriage, Sarah graduated from the city's normal school (teaching-training institute) and taught public school in Coronado, California.

Jacob Stern purchased a five-acre property bounded by Hollywood Boulevard, Vine Street, Selma Avenue, and Ivar Street from Col. Robert Northam, a wealthy inventor and manufacturer. The Stern house was described as "one of the beautiful show places of Hollywood" (Edward O. Palmer, *History of Hollywood*, page 106).

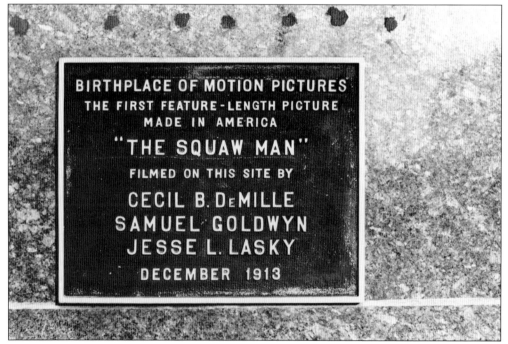

In 1912, Jacob Stern leased a two-acre portion of his property at Vine Street and Selma Avenue to the Lasky Feature Play Company, which became Paramount Pictures. In 1913, Cecil B. DeMille, Samuel Goldwyn, and Jesse Lasky made Hollywood's first feature-length film, *The Squaw Man*, at the barn on Stern's property.

Rabbi Sigmund Hecht is pictured at the center of the 1904 confirmation class at Congregation B'nai B'rith. The confirmands are, from left to right, Laurence Lewin, Stella Cohn, Victor Hecht, Henrietta Hirschfeld, Sylvan Cole, Josef Citron, Milton Lesser, Alda Danziger, Nathan Malinow, Vivian Ancker, and William Hellman.

Siegfried G. Marshutz, one of Los Angeles's first modern optometrists, was active in Jewish and civic organizations. He served on the Los Angeles Library Commission from 1905 to 1908 and resigned to assume the presidency of the Jewish Orphans Home of Southern California, which opened its doors on January 4, 1909. The organization has continued as Vista Del Mar Child and Family Services.

Born in Khoderkov, a small shtetl near Kiev, Benjamin Platt immigrated to New York City in 1902 or 1903 and worked as a salesman for the Singer Sewing Machine Company. Benjamin arrived in Los Angeles around 1906 and sold sewing machines door-to-door. He established his first store on West Seventh Street in 1909, selling sewing machines and pianos. Within two years, the store was selling only musical instruments.

In 1918, the main store of Platt Music Company was located on South Broadway. By the late 1920s, the business had expanded to 30 stores from Los Angeles to San Francisco, making it one of the four largest music chains in America. The Platt Music Company Building, a 12-story Gothic Revival structure on South Broadway, opened in 1927. When the Great Depression forced the liquidation of the Platt Music Company, Benjamin Platt salvaged the business by acquiring the music concession at the May Company.

In 1908, Benjamin Platt married Sophie Cohen, a native of Russia whom he had known in New York. Their four sons, Herman, David, Conrad, and Leo, were all born in Los Angeles. Herman, the eldest son, served as chief executive officer of Platt Music from 1956 to 1984.

Sinai Temple was chartered in 1906 as the first Conservative synagogue in Southern California. The first building was at 1153 Valencia Street, which currently houses the Pico-Union project—a multifaith cultural arts center and house of worship. In 1925, the rapidly growing congregation moved to its second building, pictured here at the corner of Fourth Street and New Hampshire Avenue in the Wilshire District. The third and current building was constructed in 1960 at 10400 Wilshire Boulevard.

The ground-breaking for the Sinai Temple building at Fourth Street and New Hampshire Avenue took place on February 15, 1925. Among those in attendance was Benjamin Platt, standing fifth from the left. Benjamin was the congregation's longest-serving president (1930–1951).

The Concordia Club's eclectic affairs included decadent dinner parties, Purim costume balls, dramatic presentations, and elaborate picnics, such as this one at Verdugo Park on May 17, 1908. The club was active until around 1915. In 1920, Rabbi Edgar F. Magnin led a well-heeled group in forming Hillcrest Country Club, which soon acquired a 142-acre plot near Beverly Hills. Early membership largely comprised the same prominent families that controlled the Concordia Club, including the Newmarks and Hellmans.

Established in 1909, the Behrendt-Levy Insurance Agency was the first to work out liability policies for the motion picture industry, beginning with the Selig Polyscope Company, Southern California's first permanent movie studio. Isaac O. Levy (left) and Sam Behrendt (right) are seen here in their office in the Union Bank Building around 1938.

In 1909, Jacob Salzman purchased the interest of his partner, Adolph Klein, in Klein & Salzman, which sold clothing and furnishing. Jacob continued the business under his own name, as seen in this photograph from around 1910.

In 1885, five-year-old Harry A. Hollzer left New York City for San Francisco with his family. The death of Harry's father in 1890 left his mother unable to care for her six children, aged two to 16. Henry and his four brothers were sent to live at the Pacific Hebrew Orphan Asylum in San Francisco, while their one sister, Esther, remained at home. Harry decided to become a lawyer during his time at the orphanage. He studied law at the University of California, Berkeley, and in 1903 was one of the school's first law graduates. Harry practiced law in San Francisco until moving to Los Angeles in 1909 and establishing the firm of Morton, Hollzer & Morton in 1912. He was appointed to the California Superior Court in 1924, replacing Judge John W. Shenk, who had been elevated to the state's supreme court. A *San Francisco Chronicle* article from May 14, 1924, quoted Harry as saying, "It was a surprise to me, for I was not a candidate."

In January 1931, Harry A. Hollzer was nominated to the US District Court for the Southern District of California by Pres. Herbert Hoover, and he served in that capacity until his death on February 14, 1946. Harry adjudicated several cases involving Hollywood celebrities, including Mae West, Hedy Lamarr, and Clara Bow, and swore in Marlene Dietrich as a US citizen in 1939.

The Young Zionists Association *Literary and Musical Entertainment will take place on Thursday Evening, April 22nd, at 8 p. m., at their meeting hall, 337½ S. Hill Street. Yourself and friends are cordially invited to attend.*

Programme

1.	Address	MR. S. G. MARSHUTZ
2.	Vocal Solo	Miss Rebecca Cohn
3.	Piano and Violin Duet	The Misses Berkowitz and
4.	Recitation	Miss Fannie Wolf
5.	Vocal Solo	Mr. Leo Jacobson
6.	Address	COL. GEO. N. BLACK

DANCING TO FOLLOW

The Social Committee have arranged for an "Evening at Home" For MEMBERS ONLY, which will take place on Thursday Evening April 29th. A paid orchestra will furnish the latest dance music and refreshments will be served.

E. M. FINKENSTEIN, Cor. Secretary

The April 22, 1909, meeting of the Young Zionist Association of Los Angeles (established in 1902) featured addresses from optometrist Siegfried G. Marshutz and Col. George N. Black, a real estate broker and owner of a large office building at Fourth and Hill Streets. Leo Jacobson, one of the program's vocal soloists, had a tailor shop on West Fourth Street.

Russian-born Isaac Henry Goldberg's family settled in Chicago in 1890. Isaac later worked in the steel business in Indiana before coming to Los Angeles in 1910. When his downtown dry goods store failed in 1913, Isaac started a junk business in the Boyle Heights area, just east of the Los Angeles River. The neighborhood was soon to become a center of Jewish life from the 1920s to the 1950s.

Isaac Henry Goldberg, his wife, Rose, and their children resided on Ganahl Street (now Fickett Street), where Isaac also ran his junk business. In 1921, the Goldbergs went to Des Moines, Iowa, and lived there for a year. Returning to California, Isaac spent a few months in the Mojave Desert buying and selling old mining machinery. With the proceeds, he opened a poultry market on Brooklyn Avenue (now Cesar Chavez Avenue) in Boyle Heights.

Dr. Herman Sugarman moved to Los Angeles after graduating from Creighton Medical College in Omaha, Nebraska, in 1910 and completing his residency at nearby St. Joseph's Hospital. He was an asthmatic with a "weak chest" and, like many others, came to Southern California for its widely touted health benefits.

Dr. Herman Sugarman became a favorite physician of upper-crust residents of Los Angeles, including Guy Cochran, head of Pacific Mutual Life Insurance, actress Jean Harlow, and presidents of major movie studios. Herman is pictured here around 1920 on his way to make a house call.

In 1911, seventeen-year-old Isadore M. Hattem, a Sephardic Jew from Constantinople, Turkey, left home for Paris, where he worked briefly in a linen shop. He next moved to Buenos Aires, Argentina, and engaged in the spice trade. After falling victim to a rare form of fever in 1913, Isadore settled in Los Angeles, a popular health destination in those days. By 1917, he was one of six Sephardic tenants operating at Grand Central Market on South Broadway. Ten years later, he opened a large store at Forty-Third Street and Western Avenue that he called a "supermarket," the first of its kind.

Rabbi Edgar F. Magnin received his ordination from the Reform movement's Hebrew Union College in 1914. Following a brief pulpit at Temple Israel in Stockton, California, Magnin was hired as assistant rabbi to Rabbi Sigmund Hecht of Los Angeles' Congregation B'nai B'rith in 1915. Magnin became the congregation's sixth senior rabbi in 1919 and served there for a total of 69 years. Known as the "Rabbi to the Stars," Magnin developed close ties with many in the motion picture and television industries.

From the time of his arrival in Los Angeles, Rabbi Edgar F. Magnin was concerned about the westward movement of the city and its Jewish community. His plans to relocate Congregation B'nai B'rith were realized in 1929 with the opening of the current building at 3663 Wilshire Boulevard. Since known as Wilshire Boulevard Temple, the building was placed in the National Register of Historic Places in 1984.

The site for Congregation Talmud Torah, better known as the Breed Street School, was purchased in 1915. The Orthodox congregation originally constructed a wood-framed school building and small synagogue at the site on 247 North Breed Street. The present building, completed in 1923, was a centerpiece of the Jewish community of Boyle Heights and nearby City Terrace through the 1950s.

BROWNSTEIN-LOUIS COMPANY.

Workers at Brownstein-Louis Company are pictured here in 1917 prior to marching in the World War I Preparedness Day parade. Henry Louis, wearing a straw hat, is seen in the front row underneath the number 6 in the address (716–722 South Los Angeles Street).

After Kaspare Cohn's death in 1916, Ben Meyer served as president of Kaspare Cohn Commercial & Savings Bank. This was a period of great economic growth in Los Angeles, and Ben had a knack for loaning money to entrepreneurs who developed successful businesses. The bank's name was changed to Union Bank & Trust Company in 1918. Ben continued as president until 1945.

This 1917 photograph, taken at a Boyle Heights movie studio, shows (from left to right) Laurence A. Lewin, Charlie Chaplin, Edna Purviance, and Ross Lewin. Edna was one of Chaplin's leading ladies, starring in *The Floorwalker* (1916), among other films. Brothers Laurence and Ross Lewin worked at the Brownstein-Louis garment manufacturing firm, which supplied the fledgling film industry and featured movie stars in its advertisements.

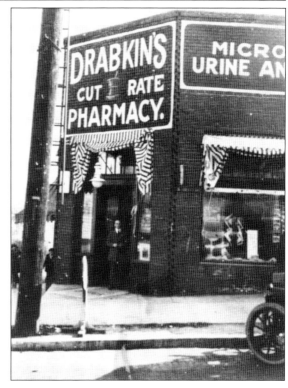

Adolphe Drabkin, pictured here with his pharmacy on Grand Avenue in 1919, was a graduate of McGill University in Montreal, Canada. A fluent speaker of French, he had a strong following among the area's French colony.

Margarete Singer is buried in the Beth Olam section of Hollywood Forever Cemetery. The cemetery, located at 6000 Santa Monica Boulevard in the Hollywood district, began as Hollywood Cemetery in 1899. By 1920, Paramount Pictures and RKO Pictures had purchased 40 acres of the 100-acre property that held no internments. A portion of the remaining land was set aside for Beth Olam Cemetery, a burial ground for members of the local Jewish community. Many notable Jews are buried at Hollywood Forever Cemetery, including actor Peter Lorre; film director Edgar G. Ulmer; Superman cocreator Jerry Siegel; film composers Franz Waxman, Eric Wolfgang Korngold, and Eric Zeisl; Paramount Pictures cofounder Jesse Lasky; bandleaders Woody Herman and Nelson Riddle; Warner Bros. Cartoons founder Leon Schlesinger; and notorious gangster Bugsy Siegel.

A parade was held in Los Angeles on June 27, 1920, to celebrate Great Britain's acceptance of the Mandate for Palestine, which had been agreed to in April 1920 at the San Remo conference in Italy. The parade stretched from the Los Angeles Courthouse to the Coliseum at Exposition Park, where a rally also took place. The crowd, estimated at over 25,000, was the largest Jewish gathering in Los Angeles to that time. Speakers included Aaron Shapiro, president of the Zionist District of Los Angeles, Jewish community leader Marco Newmark, and Rabbi Isidore Myers of Sinai Temple. This photograph shows the parade in progress, with the parade officials leading the way, followed by marchers carrying the American and Jewish flags and a brass band.

Max and Sarah Rose Broder (center) arrived in Los Angeles with their son in 1921. They took over a small music store on South Central Avenue that had living quarters in the rear. In 1922, they opened a bakery on Brooklyn Avenue (now Cesar Chavez Avenue) in Boyle Heights. The bakery's quick success attracted Louis Felhandler and Ruben Umansky, who purchased the business and renamed it Warsaw Bakery. In 1923, the Broders established a bakery and delicatessen at 2210 South Central Avenue.

Laurence A. Lewin (left) and Herman A. Politz (right) won the first President's Cup golf tournament at Hillcrest Country Club in 1923. Laurence was a buyer for the Brownstein-Louis Company, and Herman operated a fine men's clothing store. Both were charter members of Hillcrest.

Famed cantor Yosele Rosenblatt performed on the vaudeville stage at Loew's State Theatre on South Broadway in 1925. The Los Angeles engagement was arranged by siblings Fanchon and Marco Wolff. The *B'nai B'rith Messenger* of June 4, 1925, reported that the Orthodox singer "will not appear at the Saturday afternoon performance at Loew's, nor on the night of Friday, the 12th." Cantor Rosenblatt performed again in Los Angeles in 1930.

Entertainer Eddie Cantor (left) is shown here with comedian Bob Hope. Cantor arrived in Los Angeles with his wife, Ida, and daughters in 1926. He was offered the lead in the groundbreaking "talkie" *The Jazz Singer* (1927) after it was turned down by George Jessel. Cantor also turned down the role, which went to Al Jolson. Eddie Cantor became a leading Hollywood star three years later with *Whoopie*, which was shot in two-color Technicolor.

As a young man, Sid Grauman traveled with his father to Dawson City, Yukon, for the Klondike Gold Rush (1896–1899), where they became involved in entertainment. In 1900, the father and son opened Unique Theatre in San Francisco. Three years later, Sid was operating the Unique Theatre in San Jose, which presented silent movies, stock theater companies, amateur nights, and vaudeville acts. The San Jose theater was demolished in the 1906 San Francisco earthquake, sending Sid to Los Angeles, where he founded Grauman's Chinese Theatre in Hollywood in 1927.

Baron Maurice de Rothschild, head of the French house of Rothschild, visited Sid Grauman at Grauman's Chinese Theatre on May 22, 1934. The guest was treated to a special screening of *The House of Rothschild*, chronicling the rise of the European banking family.

Four

1930s–1950s

The 1930s brought anxieties to the Jews of Los Angeles. Antisemitism spiked with the Johnson-Reed Immigration Act of 1924, the Great Depression, the rise of Hitler, increased migration from the Midwest and Northeast, and the Red Scare following World War II. In 1933, the *B'nai B'rith Messenger* became the first newspaper in the United States to call for a boycott of German goods. In 1935, a mass meeting took place at the Philharmonic Auditorium to protest the treatment of Jews in Germany. By the end of the decade, members of the German-American Bund were organizing pro-Nazi rallies at Hindenburg Park, named for former German president Paul von Hindenburg, in nearby La Crescenta. The 1930s also saw the incorporation of the Los Angeles Jewish Community Council (today's Jewish Federation Council) and its fundraising arm, the United Jewish Welfare Fund. By this time, much of the city's Jewish population had begun moving westwards, taking advantage of the upward mobility afforded by New Deal programs, higher educational opportunities, the growth of the film industry, and the city's rapid industrialization. Los Angeles grew significantly after the war, with thousands of veterans and others moving west with their families. Between 1940 and 1950, the city's population increased from 1,504,277 to 1,970,358. The Jewish community grew quickly during this period, adding roughly 2,000 per month during the postwar years. Between 1945 and the end of the 1950s, Los Angeles Jewry grew from roughly 150,000 to about 400,000. New suburban synagogues and community centers accompanied this growth, aided by expanding freeway systems and sprawling new housing developments. Jewish higher education also came to the West Coast with the founding of the University of Judaism in 1947 (now American Jewish University) and the Los Angeles campus of Hebrew Union College in 1954.

Benjamin Rose arrived in Los Angeles from Philadelphia in 1930 at the age of 20. The following year, he gathered a group of his male friends to form the Society Bachelors' Fraternity, which held Sunday night dances at the Royal Palm Hotel in the West Lake Park neighborhood. The dances attracted young people from Los Angeles's Jewish neighborhoods, including Boyle Heights, West Adams, Temple Street, and Santa Monica Boulevard near Western Avenue. Attendance at the first dance was estimated at 700. Benjamin Rose changed the group's name to the Bachelors' Club in 1934 and advertised in the *B'nai B'rith Messenger*. The club's last dance took place in June 1953. This photograph, from later in the club's existence, shows (from left to right) Benjamin Rose; his wife, Kay Rose; bandleader Harry James; and Helen and Phil Goldhammer.

In 1939, the Bachelors' Club held its first annual crowning of a Yom Kippur Queen at a Yom Kippur dance, which was held in the evening following the closing services of the solemn holiday. Contestants for queen were nominated by local synagogues, youth groups, and social clubs. The winner, chosen "on the basis of popularity, beauty, education and charm," was selected by a committee headed by Benjamin Rose. Entertainment was provided by such stars as Mickey Katz, Harry James, and Woody Herman. When attendance for Yom Kippur dances outgrew the Royal Palms Hotel, the event was moved to larger venues, such as the Ambassador Hotel. The city's final Yom Kippur dance took place in 1952, and the Bachelors' Club was discontinued the following year. Two reasons are cited for the club's demise. The Royal Palms Hotel was sold to the Plumbers' Union, which had meetings on Sunday nights, and Benjamin Rose became increasingly involved in real estate and construction, leaving him little time for the club.

In February 1920, thirty-nine Turkish elders formed the Sephardic Community of Los Angeles (La Communidad Sefardi), with Rabbi Abraham Caraco as its first rabbi. In 1924, the community purchased property for a synagogue at Fifty-Second Street and Second Avenue. However, due to a shortage of funds, a synagogue was never built at that location. After selling the property in 1928, a larger site was purchased on Santa Barbara Avenue (now Martin Luther King Jr. Boulevard) in the West Adams neighborhood. The ground-breaking took place on September 1, 1931, and the temple, pictured here, was dedicated on February 21, 1932. The California-style structure was the first Sephardic synagogue in Los Angeles. The congregation, which became known as Sephardic Temple Tifereth Israel, moved to its present location at 10500 Wilshire Boulevard in 1975.

Completed in 1931, the Warner Bros. Western Theatre was intended as the flagship of the Polish Jewish brothers' theater chain. The location closed a year later and reopened in the mid-1930s as the Wiltern Theatre, named for the intersection on which it sits: Wilshire Boulevard and Western Avenue. The 12-story Art Deco building that houses the theater is on the western edge of today's Koreatown.

July 25, 1931, marked the 50th anniversary of Hamburger's Department Store, established by Asher Hamburger as the People's Store in 1881. The retail building on Eighth Street and Broadway was sold to the May Company in 1924. Pictured are Tom May and his mother (left) with Katherine and David Hamburger (right) at the symbolic opening for the store's 50th-anniversary sale.

Established by New Jersey transplants Ben, Joe, and Ruby Canter, Canter Bros. Delicatessen opened its doors in 1931 on Brooklyn Avenue in Boyle Heights. During the 1930s, upwardly mobile Jews of Boyle Heights moved westwards to such areas as the Fairfax District, West Hollywood, and the San Fernando Valley. In 1948, Ben opened Canter's Deli at 439 North Fairfax Avenue, and five years later, it moved to its current address, 419 North Fairfax Avenue, formerly the Esquire Theatre. In 1985, Los Angeles–based muralist Art Mortimer painted a seven-panel mural on the exterior wall of Canter's Deli adjacent to the parking lot. The photo-collage-style painting, known as the Fairfax Community Mural, depicts Los Angeles Jewish history from 1841 to 1985. This panel shows the original Canter Bros. Delicatessen in Boyle Heights.

Albert Einstein visited Southern California in 1931, two years before immigrating to America. In addition to visiting the California Institute of Technology in Pasadena, meeting Nobel laureate and Caltech president Robert A. Millikan, and befriending fellow pacifists Charlie Chaplin and Upton Sinclair, Einstein met with Rabbi Edgar F. Magnin of Wilshire Boulevard Temple, pictured here.

The Jewish Aeronautical Association began in 1933 with a small group of Los Angeles–based pilots. Leopold Shluker, a prosperous businessman, was inspired to organize the club after an aircraft mechanic told him that Jews could not fly airplanes. There were about 100 members between 1933 and 1941, when the club disbanded due to World War II.

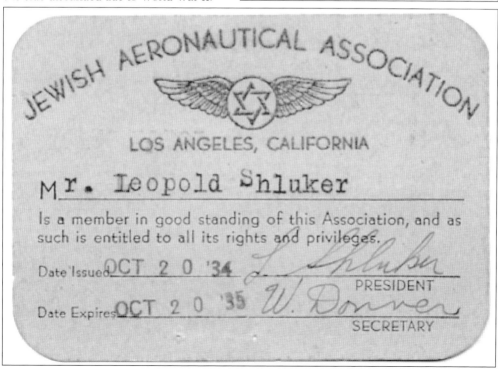

Before immigrating to America in 1923, Jacob Sonderling was rabbi of the Hamburg Temple and a chaplain in the German army during World War I. He arrived in Los Angeles in 1934 and founded the Society for Jewish Culture–Fairfax Temple. An advocate for fusing the arts and Jewish worship, Rabbi Sonderling commissioned four leading Los Angeles–based émigré composers to write Jewish works: Ernst Toch, Arnold Schoenberg, Erich Wolfgang Korngold, and Eric Zeisl.

The Los Angeles branch of the Workmen's Circle (Der Arbeter Ring) was established in 1906 to promote workers' rights, socialist ideals, Yiddish studies, and Eastern European Jewish culture. In its early days, the group acted as a mutual aid society, helping immigrant members adapt to life in America. Students are assembled outside the Workmen's Circle building for their 1934–1935 school picture.

Raphael Soriano, a Sephardic Jew born in Rhodes, Greece, immigrated to America in 1924. He settled with relatives in Los Angeles and studied architecture at the University of Southern California from 1929 to 1934. Raphael helped define a period of 20th-century architecture that became known as mid-century modern and pioneered the use of modular prefabricated steel and aluminum in residential and commercial buildings. He received his first commission in 1934 from concert pianist Helen Lipetz and her husband, Emmanuel. The house, located in the Los Feliz area of Los Angeles, is noteworthy for its semicircular music room. The house design was chosen as one of four American buildings for the 1937 International Architectural Exhibition in Paris, where it was awarded the Prix de Rome. Of the 50 buildings Soriano built, only 12 remain standing.

Founded in 1935 as the Olympic Jewish Center, Temple Beth Am is the third oldest Conservative synagogue in Los Angeles. The congregation took its present name in 1957 and, two years later, moved into a building designed by African American architect Ralph A. Vaughn. The synagogue is located on the corner of Olympic and La Cienega Boulevards, just south of Beverly Hills.

The first issue of the *Eastside Journal*, a Boyle Heights newspaper, was published on March 21, 1935. The editor, Al S. Waxman, wrote from a distinctly liberal and socially conscious point of view, at different times opposing the internment of Japanese Americans, decrying the Zoot Suit Riots, calling out antisemitism, and criticizing other forms of bigotry. Al's son, Henry Waxman, served as the US representative for California's 33rd Congressional District from 1975 to 2015.

The Juniors of Temple Tifereth Israel were formed in 1935. The group originally comprised youth from Tifereth Israel but soon included members from the Sephardic Hebrew Center, as well as several Ashkenazi members.

Judge Leo Freund was appointed to the Los Angeles Municipal Court in 1936, joining several other Jews who contributed to the city's judiciary, including Harry A. Hollzer, a federal judge; Ben Scheinman, a municipal court judge and chairman of the Boy Scouts; and Isaac Pacht, chairman of the California State Prison Board.

The Guardians of the Los Angeles Hebrew Sheltering Home for the Aged (today's Jewish Home) began with a charter dinner on May 16, 1938. The volunteer organization, which raises funds for needy seniors, developed into one of the city's major charities.

The first permanent building for the Los Angeles Jewish Home was acquired in Boyle Heights in 1916 and housed over 350 senior residents between the 1920s and 1930s. The movement of Jews to other parts of the city during the 1940s and 1950s prompted the Jewish Home to open new facilities in the San Fernando Valley. This photograph shows five residents commemorating the fall festival of Sukkot in 1940.

Temple Emanuel of Beverly Hills was established in 1938 with Ernest Trattner as its founding rabbi. Rabbi Trattner was the author of several books, including *As a Jew Sees Jesus* (1931) and *The Story of the World's Great Thinkers* (1942).

Lemuel Goldwater (left) and Morris Cohn (right) celebrated the 50th anniversary of their clothing business, Cohn-Goldwater, in April 1939. Established by Morris in 1889 as the city's first garment manufacturing firm, the business expanded when Lemuel joined in 1899. In 1909, they erected the first modern factory building in Los Angeles at San Julian and East Twelfth Streets.

Rabbi Max Nussbaum was ordained at the Jewish Theological Seminary in Breslau, Germany, in 1933, where he also earned a doctorate. He was arrested by the Gestapo in Berlin in 1936 while serving as director of the League for Jewish Culture and was later released from prison. He served as a rabbi in Berlin before coming to America at the invitation of Rabbi Stephen S. Wise of New York City. Nussbaum became the rabbi of Temple Israel of Hollywood in 1942 and remained there until his death in 1974. He authored several philosophical books and guided actress Elizabeth Taylor in her conversion to Judaism in 1959. He was also president of the Zionist Organization of America (1962–1965), an action committee member of the World Zionist Organization, and an executive member of the World Union of General Zionists. Rabbi Nussbaum is seen here speaking at Israeli prime minister David Ben-Gurion's goodwill visit to Los Angeles in May 1951.

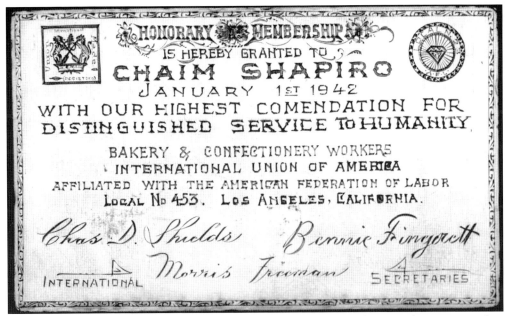

The 1930 California gubernatorial race included candidates for the Socialist Party: author Upton Sinclair for governor and Chaim Shapiro, a Russian-born attorney and Labor Zionist, for lieutenant governor. They lost in a Republican landslide. Shapiro was a graduate of the University of Southern California Law School and was instrumental in organizing the Jewish Consumptive Relief Association, which developed into City of Hope. He also ran unsuccessfully for Los Angeles mayor in 1933. In 1942, Shapiro was made an honorary member of the predominantly Jewish Bakery & Confectionery Workers International Union.

In 1943, the Boyle Heights Victory House, on the corner of Soto Street and Brooklyn Avenue (now Cesar Chavez Avenue), raised over $1 million selling war bonds and stamps. Members of the Boyle Heights War Savings Committee held an affair to celebrate the milestone at Straus Auditorium. Chaired by Harry Jaffe, the event featured stars of radio, stage, and film.

The Fairfax District, in central Los Angeles, attracted traditionally observant Jews during the 1930s and 1940s. The area's Jewish population continued to grow after World War II, necessitating new synagogues, religious schools, a Jewish community center, kosher markets and eateries, and various Jewish shops, such as the one pictured here. Today, the intersection of Fairfax Avenue and Beverly Boulevard is called Raoul Wallenberg Square, honoring the Swedish diplomat who saved thousands of Hungarian Jews from the Nazis.

Temple Isaiah was incorporated as a Reform congregation on September 12, 1947. Originally named Temple Isaiah of Culver City, the synagogue is located at 10345 West Pico Boulevard. The current building, designed by Kenneth Nels Lind, was constructed in 1954. This photograph shows the architect's model from 1951.

Solomon's Bookstore, the first Jewish bookstore in Los Angeles, was established in Boyle Heights in the 1930s by Chaya and Elimelech Solomon, emigrants from Palestine. Solomon's moved to 445 North Fairfax Avenue in 1948. Chaya and Elimelech's son Nathan, pictured here, ran the family store for many years.

Silent film star Mary Pickford, a non-Jew, was committed to the wellbeing of older Jewish residents of Los Angeles. In March 1948, the cornerstone of the five-story Mary Pickford Building was laid at the Boyle Heights campus of the Los Angeles Jewish Home for the Aged. The building was dedicated in 1952.

Mary Pickford, center, enjoyed spending time with the residents of the Jewish Home. She referred to the residents as her "babies" and related, "I have never been a 'shiksa' to them, that is, a gentile woman." She loved when they called her *mammale* (little mother).

The funeral for entertainer Al Jolson was held at Temple Israel of Hollywood on October 26, 1950. An estimated 20,000 people converged on the temple, making it one of the largest funerals in showbusiness history. George Jessel and Rabbi Max Nussbaum delivered eulogies in front of 1,500 people seated in the sanctuary. Bob Hope spoke to the crowd from Korea via shortwave radio.

Al Jolson is interred at Hillside Memorial Park Cemetery (established in 1941), the final resting place of many Jews from the entertainment industry. Jolson's widow, Erle Galbraith, commissioned his mausoleum at Hillside, which was designed by prominent African American architect Paul Williams. Next to the marble structure, consisting of a dome and six pillars, is a bronze statue of Jolson resting on one knee with arms outstretched, as if preparing to sing.

David Ben-Gurion, Israel's first prime minister, visited Los Angeles in May 1951 during his goodwill tour of American cities. Ben-Gurion (right) is seated with film producer Samuel Goldwyn and 10-year-old Sheila Beilin.

In 1952, four families met to make plans for a synagogue in Culver City, a center of film and television production just outside Los Angeles. Temple Akiba was formed the following year and affiliated with the Reform movement. In 1955, the congregation purchased a lot on Sepulveda Boulevard, procured three small buildings, and had them moved to the lot. In 1962, architect Robert Kennard was commissioned to design a new synagogue building at the site, the model of which is seen here.

Originally from Newark, New Jersey, Isadore "Dore" Schary, a playwright and motion picture director, writer, and producer, became head of production at Metro-Goldwyn-Mayer and eventually its president during the 1950s. Among his credits is the Academy Award–nominated documentary *The Battle of Gettysburg* (1955), which he wrote and produced.

Singer and dancer Sammy Davis Jr. became interested in Judaism after experiencing a near-fatal automobile accident on November 19, 1954, which caused him to lose his left eye. Entertainer Eddie Cantor, Sammy's friend, visited him in the hospital, where they discussed similarities between the Jewish and African American cultures. By the time Sammy married his second wife, Swedish-born actress May Britt, on November 13, 1960, he was known publicly as a Jew. Their interracial wedding was scheduled to take place at Temple Israel of Hollywood. However, the temple received numerous threatening phone calls, and the venue was changed to Sammy's home in the Hollywood Hills. The temple's assistant rabbi, William M. Kramer, officiated. Sammy formally converted to Judaism in 1961. He is pictured here during his widely publicized visit to Israel in 1969.

Bibliography

Aron, Stephen. *The American West: A Very Short Introduction*. New York: Oxford University Press, 2015.

Epstein, David W. *Why the Jews Were So Successful in the Wild West and How to Tell Their Stories*. Woodland Hills, CA: Isaac Nathan, 2007.

Epstein, David W., and Regina Merwin. "Western States Jewish History 40-Year Person Index." *Western States Jewish History* 40: 3-4 (2008): 349–423.

Friedmann, Jonathan L. *A City Haphazard: Jewish Musicians in Los Angeles, 1887–1927*. Washington, DC: Academica, 2017.

Rischin, Moses, and John Livingston, eds. *Jews of the American West*. Detroit: Wayne State University Press, 1991.

Rochlin, Harriet, and Fred Rochlin. *Pioneer Jews: A New Life in the Far West*. New York: Mariner, 2000.

Sass, Stephen J. *Jewish Los Angeles: A Guide*. Los Angeles: Jewish Federation Council of Greater Los Angeles, 1982.

Starr, Kevin. *California: A History*. New York: Modern Library, 2005.

Stern, Norton B., ed. *The Jews of Los Angeles: Urban Pioneers*. Los Angeles: Southern California Jewish Historical Society, 1981.

Sturman, Gladys, and David Epstein. "Postscript: The Western States Jewish History Archives." In *A Cultural History of Jews in California*, edited by Bruce Zuckerman, William Deverell, and Lisa Ansell, 47–54. West Lafayette, IN: Purdue University Press, 2009.

Szasz, Ferenc Morton. *Religion in the Modern American West*. Tucson: University of Arizona Press, 2000.

Vorspan, Max, and Lloyd P. Gartner. *History of the Jews of Los Angeles*. San Marino, CA: Huntington Library, 1970.

Walsh, Margaret. *The American West: Visions and Revisions*. New York: Cambridge University Press, 2005.

Wilson, Karen S., ed. *Jews in the Los Angeles Mosaic*. Berkeley: University of California Press, 2013.

ABOUT THE ORGANIZATION

Established in 1968, the Western States Jewish History Association (WSJHA) is dedicated to the discovery, collection, and dissemination of items and information pertaining to Jews of the region. The online Jewish Museum of the American West, a subsidiary of WSJHA, features hundreds of exhibits on the region's early Jewish pioneers.

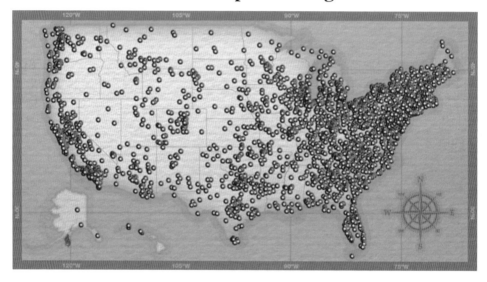